Meaning in Some Symbols from Mythology

by

Hubert J. Squires

ISBN 978-1-4303-2185-9

Dedication

This Book is dedicated to:

Stephanie N. M. Squires

Meanings In Some Symbols From Mythology

INTRODUCTION

In the present work I am searching for the basic meaning in some symbolic concepts from our human heritage, mostly from mythology, including classical Grecian, Sumerian, Biblical, Arabic and others. Day to day human living involves a lot of mythology whether it is religious or societal beliefs or even the myths of science and technology (which are subject to continual change and revision). I refer here to some of the ideas in mythology that can be expressed as a symbol or a story with some possible meanings.

What seems especially true of Greek mythological persons, objects or monsters is that they represent some psychological condition of a human. One can then guess fairly accurately at what they symbolize. I have attempted to do this with other myths as well, but anyone could equally venture a guess at a meaning different from the one I suggest. I have included at the end a bibliography of works I have consulted but not always followed. There is also an index to the names used.

It is often said that humans are the only animals that think symbolically. Language itself is symbolical, and is the mainstay of myths and human thought through distant time, and we know that its complexity of words and written characters are not used by any other animals on this planet except humans (*Homo sapiens*). Without language we would not have mythology. It is possible that our immediate pre-human ancestor (*Homo erectus (ergaster)*) also had some language skills, since they used tools and understood the use of fire, but there are no identifiable records left by them as far as we know. Could some markings on rocks be attributed to them? They lived for about one million years, and spread over much of the world known at that time, so were a very successful species, but they eventually started to change and disappeared. Our species that succeeded them (evolved from them) lived for thousands of years the way they lived, but were basically different, perhaps especially in the way we think, and we have developed records and technologies of our thinking only in comparatively recent time. Probably in the last thirty thousand years or so, if we include drawings on rocks or on cave walls. Some of the presently well known records are found in our heritage of written literature and mythology of fairly recent time.

There are other symbolic sounds and gestures that we use besides language which are easily understood by humans. But many of these (also including words) are understood by other animals such as horses and dogs. And many symbolic sounds or gestures made by other animals give meanings that are understood by us. Some symbolic sounds or gestures made by some animals are not understood by us, but which must have a lot of meaning for them, such as the songs of whales (an animal that is much further evolved than humans).

In present day society most of us grew up in a mythological setting, usually of a religious sect as followed by our parents and others in our community. We believed ours was different from the others and the only true one. But where based on books such as the Bible or Koran, the mythology was the same and our sects were all alike in basic content. As in a tribal context, everybody was happy if you accepted what they all believed and if you followed their customs and rituals. Some of the common symbols in our and other well-known mythologies are as follows.

SYMBOLS

Some of the Symbols in use by humans for many years and found in mythology are as follows. These are mostly single concepts and can be expressed sometimes in a word, a name of a mythological person and also in a phrase or sentence, or even as a story. I have taken many from Greek myths and the Bible, perhaps the richest to have survived from many years ago to the present. The meanings I suggest are tentative so other meanings are possible.

𝕲 𝕺 𝕯

One of the symbols in our heritage is of a God. This concept originated most likely before writing was used, and appears in the earliest writings of Sumeria and classical Greece, for example. Its importance is almost universal among humans and must have a basic significance. Wise men and women of ancient time realized this and created gods for themselves in recognition of this mystery and power. Some considered there was likely only one god. Since the various forms of sky gods, animalistic gods and various concepts of gods and goddesses are symbolic of something and not real entities in themselves, there must be a basic reality to these concepts of importance to us in our existence on this planet.

Apparently the reality is that **GOD** means **LIFE**.

LIFE has a mysterious quality, is tremendously powerful, is everywhere on this planet in some form, and has been instrumental in the creation and evolution of many life forms from unicellular organisms to various animals and plants on the planet earth. How life originated or where it came from we do not know. Whether it was self-generating from primordial soups or came from somewhere outside the planet is still a mystery. It is not known whether it is anywhere else outside of the planet earth, either on other planets in the solar system or in other systems. There is some evidence of organic material from comets, and also organic matter has been observed far out in the Milky Way galaxy, so life origin may have been from the cosmos. (It could not be responsible for the creation of the universe!!! The universe itself in its vastness and immense numbers of stars, etc., is something else. Perhaps it could be called "god", but it is very remote from us and has little relation to us on this relatively small planet in our solar system).

Concepts and names of GOD have varied a great deal in human societies. Some usual or well-known ones include:

1. Father gods such as Ea, Zeus (Jupiter), Jehovah, Allah and others, possibly reflecting patriarchal trends in human societies.

2. Mother goddesses such as Isis, Hera (Juno), Rhea and others possibly reflecting matriarchal trends.

Mother and Father concepts also reflect the generating aspects of advanced LIFE forms on this planet, both in plants and animals.

3. Evil or mischievous gods such as Pan, Satan, Loki and others have been invented to reflect human weaknesses or evil deeds and the bad effects of some chance events on individual humans or human societies.

Also where there were ideas of a panoply of Gods as in classical Greece, each god had special human characteristics, such as the musical ability of Apollo or care of the environment of Artemis, and they all had human weaknesses as well. Even where a one god was envisaged, as in Jehovah, a human weakness (jealousy) was presumed as a characteristic.

Concepts of gods have been the basis of religions, although there are some religions without primary reference to gods (such as Zen Buddhism) but with a basic reference to LIFE.

HEAVEN

Since Heaven or its opposite, Hell, are not places in the sky or in the earth, the basic meaning must be in the way humans think. Ideas of beautiful places where gods live have been common ideas for thousands of years, and in many religions such places are thought to be where we go when we die. The reality of these concepts are concepts and no more. But they are a part of our heritage of mythology and have a meaning of value to us. Like other animal or plant life species, our existence as individuals is apparently limited to one life cycle.

HEAVEN is basically conceptual, or a State of MIND

The way we think or feel about ourselves or how we are able to think, imagine or are aware of the greatness and sublimeness of existence represents our "kingdom of heaven", as taught by Jesus in the New Testament of the Bible ("The kingdom of God is within you"). How to achieve a "kingdom of God" is a maturing in our way of thinking as we develop our individual way of looking at life. This seems to change or grow through our living experiences and adjustments in our ways of thinking and feeling.

We like to think that the human mind that has produced many ideas in a lifetime has a continuing existence, at least in the form of these ideas, and most certainly many of the ideas continue to exist to be worked on by other human minds, if they are recorded and can be adapted to various uses. Perhaps some of the concepts of "heaven" through the ages arose from this realization.

Great teachers or philosophers have stressed that every individual mind has its own "kingdom of heaven" or way of thinking or philosophy. This is apparently an attribute of present day humans (*Homo sapiens)* and should be respected in every individual human from birth to maturity, since every single one is unique and may be considered to have something to contribute (in some way; even though possibly not easily understood).

Our sense of beautiful places or beauty in any form is part of our enjoyment of life leading to the sublime or heaven of our existence.

On the other hand the despondency we feel in the midst of catastrophic chance events, or difficult conditions we may have to suffer, represent a HELL of torment or the opposite to the bliss of our HEAVEN.

The symbolic representations of these feelings or ideas have been recognized through the ages and represented by such terms. With such concepts the human can exercise some control to make life understandable and workable as far as is possible for any individual human.

ANGELS

What do we do with our angels from Heaven? What comes from our heavens or states of mind are THOUGHTS. Our "Comforting Angels" are therefore our comforting thoughts.

ANGELS = THOUGHTS

Thoughts come often and sometimes fleetingly. They are the messengers of the ideas we need to be aware of or to do anything.   The mind is continually in action even when we are asleep,   and we are likely to be directing thoughts to get something done or even to rest when we need to.

When the mythical biblical person Jacob meets a host of "angels", they are his multiple thoughts when confronted with the presence of his brother Esau. Esau is said to have a company of four hundred men, and Jacob had reason to be concerned about how Esau thought of what he had done to appropriate the blessing and birthright due him from his father. Jacob needed to wrestle with his fears or misgivings, and to come to a conclusion about who he was and what he had accomplished for his brother to be reconciled to him and with what he had done -- he wrestled with an angel (his main thought) all night. His conclusion was that he was basically an "Israel"(prince) and not a "Jacob"

(supplanter).

"On wings of thought" is an expression personified by the winged angels of our mythology.

Of course the "bad angels" that have "fallen from heaven" can be none other than the wrong ideas or thinking we may sometimes give way to.   It is not easy to recognize sometimes that what we are thinking is wrong. Or we may give way to what other people think is wrong. When we think of doing harm or evil to other humans, we know that it is wrong.

As in the Bible, when Jacob slept by the ladder of his dreams, the angels going up were his optimistic thoughts about his journey, while those coming down represented his thoughts of fear and pessimism about what might happen on his journey.

MOTHER MARY = GENERATION PRINCIPLE

This respected religious figure is basically representative of the principle of generation in many life forms including both plants and animals. Goddesses which represented advanced forms of life generation were Isis, Ceres and others.

JESUS AS GOD = MOST ADVANCED CONSCIOUS LIFE FORM

This respected religious figure is basically representative of the most advanced conscious life form (human) on this planet. Although humans are not the most highly evolved of animals, they are the ones with the greatest mental ability. Some other humans representative of a high consciousness in our recorded history were Guatama (Buddha), Mohammad , and many others if we consider our great women and men, some of whom are in our recorded history.

GARDEN OF EDEN = HUMAN EXISTENCE AS CHILD

A "Garden of Eden" existence suggests a time in our lives of early childhood when we were completely cared for and had not learned very much. But the SERPENT of understanding creeps into our consciousness, and we become aware of things and of how pleasant and stimulating is the APPLE of knowing.

The ADAM of our physical self and the EVE of our intelligence and intuitions are the realities of our existence, and we begin to be a person and no longer can stay in our primal Garden of Eden. As we grow and learn, some acquired wisdom (the "serpent" of the mythology) helps us to see what we need to do to take our place in our family and society. We have to be doing things that are also important to our own self-development as individuals.

As we grow and start trying various ways of behaving to fit in with what people expect of us, we have to be productive, whether in doing what is needed to live in our social group or to benefit our own development. We have to make choices among the different ways of living we see before or around us.

Choices of ways of living or behaviour are symbolized in the story in the Bible of Cain and Abel, for example. CAIN is a materialistic way we may be inclined to follow and ABEL not so. These propensities are within all of us. The Cain way may suppress ("kill") the Abel way at first, but most of us moderate it to live with consideration of the needs of others in our social way of living. The appearance of SETH in the myth suggests that we may go back to the "Abel" way after all, rather than be forced to follow the "Cain" way if we decide to change.

THE ARK AND THE FLOOD

This item in the mythology of the Bible may have been borrowed from the Sumerian or Greek myths of a FLOOD, since they would probably have been known by the writer or writers of the first five books of the Bible by the Hebrews, especially while in their 80 year captivity in Babylon. The story was considerably modified and may have more significance to us in a personal way.

THE ARK = A PERSONAL OUTLOOK OR PHILOSOPHY

The dimensions of the Ark and what it was meant to contain or save indicate a full and measured way of looking at any aspect of living,   including problems of various kinds we have to solve or live with in everyday life. It may be considered a Way of Life we have to decide on at some time in our individual existence.

THE FLOOD = CRITICISM BY OTHERS OF OUR "ARK"

Our ideas of how we live or what we like to do with our lives may suit us but they don't necessarily please other people.   Some major things we do may get a lot of criticism: a flood of contrary ideas to our way of thinking that may last a long time and be difficult to overcome.   To rise above them may be a personal achievement of high merit to us as individuals. We need to maintain our own ideals and way of thinking in spite of what other people may say.

RAINBOW = MANY WAYS OF LOOKING AT THINGS

The great number of prismatic colours in the rainbow (as also in the "coat of many colours" of Joseph in the Bible) represent variety in ways of thinking about things such as in ways to solve problems. It shows multiple aspects of living.

TOWER OF BABEL = RELIGIONS HUMANS HAVE CREATED

This short myth is apparently not about languages which develop normally wherever there is an isolated group of humans. It appears to be about religions.

Religions have a basis similar for all like the base of a tower. They are mainly to get people to think and behave ethically in society. But as each one is built on various principles, according to personal opinions or the strong philosophy of some avatar, so differences start to happen half way up the tower, and eventually the religions no longer appear the same and confusion among them occurs. People who follow them no longer understand each other and they cannot work together. Towards the top of the tower it becomes difficult to build because of many different ideas of how it should be done and what it should be made of.

PYRAMID = EXISTENCE, RISING ABOVE DIFFICULTIES

The pyramid was used in ancient Egypt in the building of burial tombs for pharaohs, and also in the Mayan and other cultures of Central America. It is a common mathematical figure, sometimes used to strengthen built structures. In Egyptian lore it represented existence and a defeat of death. It also symbolized ascension of the pharaohs to the sun-god after death and burial. Its shape is reminiscent of the rays of the sun.

ISIS = DEVOTION, MOTHERING

Isis became the chief goddess of the Egyptians. She had power over life and death and resurrection. Every living thing was thought to be a drop of her blood. She restored her husband, Osiris, to life when he had been killed and cut in pieces by the forces of evil. She was worshipped by all peoples of the Mediterranean area at some time in the past.

OSIRIS = REBIRTH, REINTERGRATION

Osiris, the husband of Isis, was primarily an agrarian god symbolizing the importance and power of plant life. His brother Set, an evil god, killed and dismembered him and set him adrift on the Nile. But Isis sought and found him and restored him to life. He was identified with the Sun and continuance of birth and rebirth as in plants.

HORUS = VIGILANCE, JUSTICE

Horus, the son of Isis and Osiris, was representative of the eye of justice and the victory over forces of darkness and evil. He is represented as a falcon-headed god and his emblem is a solar disc with falcon's wings. He was successful against Set, the god of evil, and was an example of vigilance against falling into sin or the snares of the enemy. Like the falcon, nothing escaped his eye.

SET = EVIL, CHAOS

Set was the brother of Osiris but jealous of him and determined to do him harm.   In fact he killed and cut him into pieces thinking therefore to destroy him.   He was representative of misdirected forces to cause evil or harmful events in the lives of people.   Powers of nature are sometimes deemed to be chaotic or dangerous if not understood.

PHOENIX = REGENERATING

The phoenix was a mythological bird capable of being reborn from its own ashes after it had burnt on a funeral pyre.   In ancient Egypt it was emblematic of the daily cycle of the sun and also the annual flooding of the river Nile and spring planting.

APSU , TIAMAT = WATERS OF SUMERIAN CREATION MYTH

From Sumerian mythology, this hits close to the mark, since life in its various forms on this planet required water (a liquid medium) to exist and develop or evolve.   Apsu was fresh water and Tiamat represented the salt seas, but Tiamat the "Abyss-Mother" was also a monster who attacked the gods in the Sumerian and Babylonian mythology of creation.   The gods gave power to Marduk to overcome Tiamat.

MARDUK = COMPETENCE, POWER

Marduk was born in the sweet waters of Apsu as the myth says.   He was asked by the gods to defend them from Tiamat. He agreed if they would give him all the power he needed. He attacked Tiamat and her followers. With the help of wind he distended Tiamat and split her in two with his sword. Part of her he made into the seas and part into the land and sky. He defeated and bound her followers including her husband Kingu. Marduk represented the sun in its renewal of planting time after the spring equinox

KINGU = CHAOTIC BUT GENERATING

Kingu, the husband of Tiamat, had been defeated and bound by Marduk. When the gods decided to make humans they wanted to use one of themselves, but since Kingu was already bound and at their mercy, they decided to use him. Ea, one of the chief gods, slew him and used his blood to make humans.

INANNA, QUEEN OF HEAVEN= COMFORTING OF HUMANS, GAIETY

Inanna was a goddess of the Sumerian people. She was thought to have lived among humans and helped them in many ways. Her sister, Ereshkigal, on the other hand was thought to live in the underworld and to taunt Inanna for living a life of pleasure with humans. But the story was that Inanna went to the underworld to show she could understand the dark side of life. She was abused but had told others of her planned journey beforehand and was rescued from the death her sister had sanctioned. She came back to live among her people.

ERESHKIGAL = MEANNESS, CRUELTY, JEALOUSY

Ereshkigal, the sister goddess of Inanna, ruled the underworld in Sumerian myth. She was jealous of her sister and treated her cruelly when she visited the underworld (to show she could take the dark side of life). Ereshkigal represented unreasonableness and cruelty.

DEMONS = INTERFERENCE, PESSIMISM, INDECISION

Destructive chance events causing chaos of one kind or another or harm to humans were often considered to be initiated by the mythical creatures of demon or devil. In effect any such initiation was by humans themselves. It is easy to blame others.

GIANTS = LARGENESS OF NATURE

Nature is so much greater than we are. It requires co-operation for the most part, and it may be made use of advantageously in many ways. In mythology and folklore giants were often killed or overcome in some way. But their dead bodies were rarely disposed of!! Killing the giant would sometimes mean getting rid of an addiction or removing a natural hindrance to some project.

MOUNTAINS = IDEALS

In myths mountains are often shown as impossible to climb, are of glass or steeper than hills, but the hero can reach the top by some, often implausible, means. Reaching the summit of a mountain could be a goal to be

achieved by courage, learning and persistence.
Mountains were represented as remote and sometimes
places where dangerous beings lived; places to be
reached by the adventurous person who would overcome
the difficulties.

GARDENS OF PLENTY = TEMPTING LUXURIES

When these gardens appear in myths there is a
suggestion and an outcome of giving way to ease and
forgetting the need to continue a quest or important task.

LIMITLESS SEA = CONTINUOUS FOUNTAIN OF IDEAS

Mythology often equates water with intellectual
possibilities. Seas in particular, because they are so
large, present endless thought opportunities as well as
dangers.

GILGAMESH = DIGNITY, AMBITION

Gilgamesh was an accomplished ruler in Sumerian
mythology. He made friends with a wild man he called
Enkidu. But after many adventures together Enkidu
died. Gilgamesh longed for immortality but eventually
realized it was impossible. In the original construction of
the myth he may have been considered as representative
of an ideal human way of life, but as a ruler he would
have had many responsibilities.

PLANT OF IMMORTALITY = DESIRING TO LIVE FOREVER

This predicts, however, the futility of a life that could go on forever. Gilgamesh in Sumerian myth desired immortality after his friend, Enkidu, died. But after finding the plant he unintentionally allowed it to be taken and eaten by a serpent. He was not convinced it would be effective.

UNDERWORLD = DARKNESS OR DISASTERS OF CHANCE EVENTS

Human life appears subject to various tragedies and often catastrophic events. These were sometimes blamed on influences from a dark realm of demons, etc., the hells of mythology. It was also imagined as a place of the dead. Death is nothing more than the end of a life.

GODS = LIFE FORCES FOR GOOD

Happy occasions often were ascribed to gods with humanlike qualities giving their bounty of good fortune (fortunate chance events), especially in Greek mythology.

HEAVEN AND EARTH = IMAGINATION AND WORK

Imagination and ideals are needed to achieve greatest accomplishments in human activity. Heaven and Earth are sometimes equated with the "Mind" and "Body" of humans in myths.

DARKNESS AND LIGHT = UNKNOWING AND KNOWING

Lack of awareness is like being in the dark, but being aware lets in the light in human ways of thinking and living. In the evolution of humans the development of a large brain enabled thinking at a much higher level than in other animals. The ability of humans to understand complex ideas is like having light to see rather than being in the dark of not seeing or understanding.

HERBS AND FRUITS OF MYTH = IDEAS AND PROJECTS TO BE WORKED ON

Practical things to do or concepts to be worked on are aspects of human activity in everyday life.   These are sometimes represented by plants in mythology where we can make use of those essential for our food and other processes.

TREES IN GARDEN OF EDEN = BRANCHING CIRCULATORY OR OTHER SYSTEMS IN BODILY FUNCTIONS

The Garden of Eden, as an orchard,   is suggested as representing the human body with its branching circulatory and nervous systems to all body parts like the branches of trees.   As suggested, however, it could represent also the phase in our lives as children.

FIRE AND BRIMSTONE = STRONG EMOTION, EXTREME ANGER

In myths "fire" or "burning" suggest strong emotional reactions of humans, mostly expressing extreme anger or upset. The myth of the destruction of Sodom and Gomorrah by fire and brimstone suggests strong emotions involved in the overcoming of an addiction.

SMOKING FURNACE = LACK OF ENTHUSIASM FOR A PROJECT

Because the furnace is smoking and not functioning properly, the indication in the myth is that the will to do best in a project could be lacking.

A MOVING LIGHTED LAMP = ZEAL TO DO SOMETHING

The well-functioning lighted lamp suggests enthusiasm for doing one's best in a project.

SACRIFICE TO THE LORD = PRESENTING WORK TO AN AUTHORITY FOR APPROVAL

In the myth the Sacrifice is put on an altar, as in a religious sense, but it is like a work being presented for approval. If not approved or accepted it could be devastating to the human.

FAMINE = LACK OF FOOD OR MATERIAL TO WORK ON

It is devastating if material to work on is not available to the worker.

FLOCK OF SHEEP = IDEAS OR MATERIAL TO WORK ON

Sheep have been amenable to herding and domestication for many years and can be representative of a workable medium.

FLOCK OF GOATS = IDEAS OF PRACTICAL ACTIVITY

Goats seem to be representative of independent or personal solving of problems and work ethic.

BULL = DIFFICULT PROBLEM

In myths meeting or dealing with a bull is always a struggle and not always successful.   Overcoming the "bull" was a physical achievement, but often meant it was a way to make something useful.

ENKIDU, THE WILD MAN = PRIMITIVE WAY OF THINKING OR LIVING

Few or no humans can live in a natural state where they are not influenced by others in their way of thinking and behaving. Humans are basically social in their way of living. Enkidu who lived among wild animals was persuaded to live among people by Gilgamesh, and became his best friend.   He had changed by associating with humans and was no longer accepted by his animal friends.

SPHINX = PROBLEM DESTROYING THE INDIVIDUAL

The Sphinx was a monster who asked a riddle most people could not solve and then killed them. Oedipus solved the riddle and the sphinx destroyed itself. Some of the problems of life such as incurable disease can destroy a person. But sometimes the disease can "destroy" itself (where it is caused by the immune system).

OEDIPUS = REJECTING GUILT, UNWITTING WRONGDOING

The father of Oedipus feared he would be killed by his son , as the Oracle had foretold, so he took his just-born son and abandoned him on a mountain, expecting him to die. But he was found by a shepherd and taken to his king who brought him up. When he left this home as a man he went to Thebes, a nearby city, but on his way met a chariot with men who brusquely ordered him out of the way. He killed the charioteer for the insult and the man with him met his death from the runaway horses. This man was his father who had been king of Thebes. The people then chose Oedipus to be their king. But it was the custom for a succeeding king to marry the Queen. Oedipus did not know she was his mother. In the following years they had three children. When Oedipus knew the facts he blinded himself. His mother killed herself. He was harried by the Erinnyes for causing the deaths of his parents (although unwittingly) and fled from them and their punishments.

LAIUS = FEARFUL, GULLIBLE

Laius was king of Thebes. He believed the oracle predicting he would be killed by his son. When his son was born he therefore abandoned him on a mountain expecting he would die there. The son was Oedipus, rescued and brought up in a neighbouring kingdom. As a man on his way toThebes, he accidentally was the cause of his father's death.

IOCASTE (JOCASTA) = VICTIMIZED BY CUSTOM

Iocaste was the mother of Oedipus and queen of Thebes. When her husband -- the king -- was killed it was the custom for a queen to re-marry the succeeding king, and she married Oedipus not knowing he was her son. When she discovered this she committed suicide.

ANTIGONE = COMFORTING, SUPPORTIVE, DUTIFUL

Antigone was the daughter of Oedipus and Iocaste. When Oedipus blinded himself and wandered helplessly away from Thebes, he was rejected by his two sons and the people, but his daughter Antigone accompanied him and helped him survive. She led him to the kingdom of Theseus at Athens where he was able to live for some time although harried by the Erinnyes

TEIRESIAS = FORETELLING, INTUITIVE

Teiresias was a seer of Thebes. When asked why the city was beset by plagues, he understood the problem of Oedipus and his mother Iocaste, and decreed that Oedipus must be sacrificed to placate the gods for the incest he had committed, even though he was not guilty intentionally.

ECHIDNE = BEASTLY, MONSTROUS

Echidne was a monster, part woman and part viper. She was the wife of Typhon and mother of the Sphinx, Cerberus, Orthrus and the vulture that tore at the liver of Prometheus.

ORTHRUS = GUARDING, WATCHFUL

Orthrus was the two-headed watchdog of the cattle of Geryon. Heracles had to kill him to take the cattle as part of his Tenth Labour.

GERYON = DEVOTION, ENTHUSIASM

Geryon was the son of Chrysaor, the warrior born from the body of Medusa when killed by Perseus. He had three heads and three bodies joined at the waist He was reputed to have great strength. He owned a herd of red cattle on the red island of Erytheia. Hercules was required to take and bring back the cattle to Eurystheus as his Tenth Labour. The recurrence of the number three in Geryon suggests his subject was religion. Also the red colour suggests enthusiasm and devotion to his subject.

The Labour of Heracles might indicate his having to teach Geryon's subject for a time.

PEGASUS = "FLIGHTS OF FANCY" -- IMAGINATION

Pegasus was a horse with wings giving it flight capability. It was born from Medusa the Gorgon when she was killed by Perseus. Medusa represented intelligence as indicated by her name which means "cleverness". Pegasus was fathered by Poseidon, god of the sea. A flying horse presents an impossible concept that can only be imaginative.

CHRYSAOR = CONFLICT OF MINDS

Chrysaor was a warrior born fully armed from Medusa the Gorgon when she died. He had been procreated by Poseidon and Medusa, both referring to intellectual pursuits but in conflict situations, as indicated by their present progeny being fully armed.

MEDUSA = INTELLECTUAL SKILL ACHIEVED, CLEVERNESS

Medusa had been a beautiful goddess but was changed by Athene, the goddess of wisdom. Looking at her face caused people to be turned into stone in the Greek myth, indicating the power of intellectual gifts to influence people. Athene was one of the Olympic gods accepted by the people, who rejected former gods and goddesses such as Medusa. Also Athene's temple had been violated by Medusa and Poseidon and she had then vented her anger on Medusa by making her ugly.

PERSEUS = INITIATIVE, DECISIVE

Perseus was famous in Greek myths for killing Medusa, one of the Gorgons, but he also saved his mother from abuse, and Andromeda, his future wife, from a sea monster. He therefore showed his decisiveness in his choices to take action especially in his defense of his mother and his future wife, and also in his defeat of the tyrant king of Seriphos.

CASSIOPEIA = SELF-CENTERED, PROUD

Cassiopeia had boasted she and her daughter were more beautiful than the Nereids thus offending them. Poseidon, their protector, therefore sent a monster to harass and kill her subjects (she was queen of Joppa), and to prevent this her daughter, Andromeda, agreed to be sacrificed to the monster. She was chained to a cliff for the monster who approached from the sea. Perseus killed the monster by exposing the head of Medusa to its sight and it was turned to stone.

ANDROMEDA = SELF-SACRIFICING, DUTIFUL

Andromeda agreed to be the victim of a sea monster sent by Poseidon because of the boast of her mother, Cassiopeia. She was chained to a cliff to await the monster. Perseus, returning from his visit to the island of the Gorgons, saw her, resolved to set her free and marry her. Her mother and father agreed (her mother reluctantly when the monster had been killed). When the monster was turned to stone, Andromeda was freed from her chains and agreed to marry Perseus and return home with him.

ORESTES = DUTIFUL, FAITHFUL

Orestes was the son of Agamemnon, the chief king of Mycenae. He was advised by Apollo to kill his mother and her lover because they had treacherously slain his father. He was pursued by the Erinnyes because of this, but eventually they relented because he had only done his duty according to custom.

ERINNYES (FURIES) = REGRETS, SELF-TORTURE

The Erinnyes beat with their scourges anyone who killed a parent, particularly a mother. They were dog-headed and with bat wings. They particularly harassed Orestes who had killed his mother, Clytaemnestra, to avenge the murder by her of his father Agamemnon. They represent how one may torture oneself or rue what one had done.

CHIMAERA = CHANGEFUL

The Chimaera was a beast with a tripartite body -- the head of a goat, the body of a lion and the hind part a serpent. It represented aspects of a three part Greek calendar year of Goat, Lion and Serpent. The Lion represented Spring, the Goat = Summer and the Serpent = Winter. The lion and goat are included in the presently accepted Zodiac where each of the twelve months in the annual cycle are represented by an animal or other symbol.

SCYLLA = CONSUMING, BITING

Scylla was a monster with six heads. It was hidden in the recesses of a cliff overlooking the sea. When ships swung too close to the cliff it darted out its six heads and seized six men of the crew who were within reach. It did this to the crew of the ship of Odysseus. Its punishment was for lack of caution.

CHARYBDIS = PULLING DOWN, SWALLOWING

Charybdis was a whirlpool in the sea. It had tremendous force and could draw down a ship into the depths until it was wrecked and all the crew drowned. Lack of caution could result in harm.

CHAOS = SHAPELESSNESS, PASSIVITY

Chaos indicates a complete lack of organization of anything; also a passive condition of human life. It suggests passivity because nothing is being done when conditions are chaotic. It was the prior condition of existence in the creation myth of the Bible and in Sumerian mythology.

HARPIES = SPITEFUL, VEXING

The Harpies were winged monsters bringing torment to humans, such as through snatching food or fouling it. They symbolized viciousness in the torments they inflicted especially the torments of guilt or depression of a human. They also provoked evil-doing. In the myth they could be driven away only by representatives of the winds, such as Boreas (the north wind), who had flight capability to match theirs, indicating ability to dispel or conquer depression, etc., in a human.

CERBERUS = TERROR,

Cerberus was a monstrous dog with three heads. It guarded the gates of Tartarus, the place of the dead, and prevented any living thing from entering or the dead from escaping. It could be called "the Hound of Hell". It represented a primitive religious belief long outmoded and that should be discarded. It was greatly disturbed when brought into the sunshine, showing that it was part of a belief that could not stand the "light of day".

E R I S = STRIFE

Eris, goddess of strife, was the twin sister of Ares, the god of war, and child of Hera and Zeus the Olympian chief gods. She pitted the pride of the three goddesses: Hera, Athene and Aphrodite against each other by their being judged which was the fairest. This eventually led to the mythical war against Troy and its destruction.

AUTOLYCUS = THIEVERY

Autolycus was a master thief, mostly stealing cattle. Hermes had given him the ability to change the colour and appearance of cattle, so the owner could no longer recognize them. Sisyphus, however, was able to circumvent this by marking his cattle's hooves with his initials so he was able to recover them.

HECATE = SORCERY, GHOSTLY

Hecate was the goddess of the dead. She was invoked by witches at crossroads. She was a fertility goddess and protectress of sailors and farmers in her benevolent aspect, but had an infernal aspect, a goddess of night-terrors.

STYX = HATED

The Styx was a river near the gateway to Tartarus, the place of the dead in Greek mythology. To cross the black muddy rivers Acheron and the Styx, Charon, the ferryman, gave passage to those who could pay, so left souls who couldn't pay to wander helplessly forever. It was the custom to leave money with the dead before burial.

NAUPLIUS = GUIDING, STEERING

Nauplius was a son of Poseidon and Anymone and became a famous navigator. He discovered the method of steering by the Great Bear and Polaris. He was the father of Palamedes, killed by the Greeks through the treachery of Odysseus. He took part in the cruise of the Argo with Jason to obtain the Golden Fleece.

PALINURUS = PILOTING

Palinurus was the steersman for the ship of Aeneas on the way to Italy. In return for a promise to allow the ship to reach its goal, Poseidon required one life and the victim chosen was Palinurus. As he watched the stars holding the helm, Poseidon came and asked him to take a rest, but he refused. However, he was overcome by sleep and fell overboard still holding the helm and was drowned.

NEMESIS = REPRISAL

Nemesis was a daughter of Oceanus and she was a goddess. She scourged and humiliated men who boasted of riches but gave nothing to the gods or to alleviate poverty. She originally was a human, Leda, who with Zeus were the parents of Helen, the cause of the Trojan war.

POLYPHEMUS = BRUTISH

Polyphemus was a son of Poseidon. He was a gigantic Cyclops (with one eye in the middle of his forehead) with a taste for the raw flesh of humans. He killed and ate six sailors of Odysseus when they entered his cave expecting hospitality as they journeyed towards home from Troy. He had once been a smith but was now a shepherd. Odysseus took vengeance on him by burning out his eye, but his curse led to the loss of all men and ships of Odysseus on his way home.

SIREN = ENTICING, FATAL ATTRACTION

The sirens were monsters, part women and part bird or fish. In the sea they looked beautiful and they sang beautiful songs to lure sailors who could not resist trying to join them in the sea. They devoured sailors who reached them. They represented the self-destruction of uncontrolled desire.

TANTALUS = UNSATISFIED CRAVING

Tantalus tried to act as a god, offering a feast to the Olympic gods, but including his son as part of the feast. He was punished for this by being fettered eternally, and although able to see water and fruits was never able to reach them to quench his thirst and allay his hunger. (We owe to him the word "tantalize").

LOTUS = ATTRACTANT, DESIRE, ADDICTION

The lotus given to the crews of the ships of Odysseus left them in a dream state in which they forgot their duties and homes and had to be forced back to their ships in chains.

SCAMANDER = INTELLECTUAL CONFLICT

The Scamander was a river near Troy that resisted the efforts of Achilles in his battle with the young men of Troy he was killing and throwing in the river. The river would have overcome Achilles but he was saved by the gods Athene and Poseidon. River gods also were common in Greek myth.

CENTAUR = DUALITY OF HUMAN NATURE, INSTINCT AND INTELLIGENCE

The centaurs were part horse and part human. Essentially they represented skilled horsemen, but they became drunk if they had wine and were often violent at these times. One of them, Chiron, was a great teacher and friend of humans.

GUARDIAN DRAGON = FORBIDDEN ACCESS TO KNOWLEDGE

In myths the dragon often guarded treasure. It was the task of humans to slay the dragon and obtain the treasure for all to enjoy. This is a typical work to be done for the benefit of all such as volunteers might do.

FIRE-BREATHING DRAGON = STRONG EMOTION (ANGER), TO AN A DDICTION (FOR EXAMPLE)

To slay the dragon was always a necessary responsibility of the hero for protection of other humans. The individual can overcome with help the ravages of addictions, but a strong commitment is necessary.

GOLDEN BOUGH = ALLOWING ACCESS TO KNOWLEDGE

The Golden Bough was from a tree dedicated to the goddess Aphrodite. It was used by Aeneas to gain entrance to the Elysian Fields, or place of the dead, to meet and talk with his father, Anchises, about his future.

CADUCEUS = EQUILIBRIUM, HEALING

The caduceus was a staff entwined with twin serpents used by Hermes (Mercury) as physician, and by Asclepius, the physician.

ASCLEPIUS = PHYSICIAN, RESTORING

Asclepius was the son of Apollo and a human, Coronis. He was taught medicine by Chiron, the centaur, and achieved such efficiency he was able to cure people of almost any disease and even restore life to the dead. Hades, god of the underworld, complained to Zeus about being cheated of the dead by Asclepius and Zeus killed him.

SIBYL = FORESIGHT, FORETELLING

The Sybils were Apollo's priestesses who had the presumed power to foretell events. In the myth of Aeneas a Sybil helped him to reach the Elysian Fields where he could ask his father, Anchises, to foretell the future of his projected city and empire, Rome

THE HOLY GRAIL = COMPASSION (CARE FOR OTHERS)

The symbols associated with the Holy Grail and their equivalents are as follows:

	Tarot	Playing Cards	Meaning
The Grail	Cups	Hearts	COMPASSION
Sword	Swords	Spades	JUDGEMENT
Salver	Pentacles	Diamonds	FIVE SENSES
Spear	Wands	Clubs	INTUITION

The quest for the Holy Grail was to obtain it to cure people of incurable diseases. It also represented a task worthy of a knight and to bring him honour and renown.

KNIGHTS ERRANT = QUEST OF A KNIGHT TO DO GOOD

In the legends of King Arthur knights went on quests for adventures that would help people in difficulty. This often resulted in the removal of oppressors or criminals who preyed on people with no means of defense. It sometimes led to the defeat and death of the knight himself.

ROUND TABLE = IMPARTIAL, EQUALITY

The Round Table at King Arthur's court gave equal representation to each one of his knights who occupied specified seats at the Table.

GALAHAD = PERFECTION

Galahad was the perfect knight in King Arthur's court. There were no blemishes in his character. He had unusual ability as a knight -- no one could defeat him in combat and he spent his life in doing good for society.

PERSEVAL = ASPIRING, COMPASSIONATE

Perseval began his knighthood as an amateur , but he had unusual ability and was ultimately successful in his quest for the Holy Grail. He shared his success with the knights Galahad and Bohort and the Lady, his sister.

KING ARTHUR = SPIRITUAL AUTHORITY

King Arthur was ruler of a Welsh kingdom and Britain (Logris), but also leader of knighthood in its greatest aspirations and achievements for goodness among peoples of his time. He instituted the Round Table where were seated the greatest knights of his time.

MERLIN = SORCERY, SUPERNATURAL POWER

Merlin was a sorcerer given to helping King Arthur achieve difficult objectives by ethical means over the black magic exerted by other sorcerers of the time. He taught much of his secrets to the Lady of the Lake who betrayed him.

LAUNCELOT = GREAT STRENGTH, ADVENTUROUS

Launcelot was the greatest knight of the Round Table in prowess and valor during combat and on quests to help the oppressed and harried people of his time. His love for Guenevere, the wife of King Arthur, was a weakness leading eventually to his disgrace.

MODRED = TRAITOROUS, REBELLIOUS

Modred, a nephew of King Arthur, assumed the kingship when the king was out of the country. He spread false news that Arthur had been killed. In the battles following King Arthur's return both were killed.

MORGANA = ENCHANTRESS

Morgana, the sister of King Arthur, exercised her enchantments in concert with Viviane, the Lady of the Lake. They received King Arthur on a barge in the lake when he died.

VIVIANE = ENTRAPMENT, DECEITFUL

Viviane, the Lady of the Lake, learned much of the magic arts from Merlin. However, she took command of him as he slept, and he was unable to continue his services to Arthur and mankind. She had previously nurtured Launcelot at the Lake and was one of the three women receiving King Arthur when he died.

GUENEVERE = LOVING

Guenevere was the wife of King Arthur. She was revered by the knights of the Round Table, but had a relationship with Launcelot, leading finally to her condemnation and sentence to death. Launcelot prevented this by rescuing her and taking her to his castle. The resulting conflicts devastated the knights and court of Arthur. Guenevere at the last retreated to a nunnery.

SISYPHUS = FUTILITY OF DECEIT OR CRIME

Sisyphus was so clever he even played tricks on the Olympic gods as well as betraying their secrets. In death his punishment was to roll a large stone to the top of a hill but it then rolled back and he had to roll it up again in perpetuity.

SYMBOLIC STORIES

The following myths such as the Labours of Heracles (Hercules) and Theseus and the voyages of Odysseus (Ulysses) and Sindbad the Sailor are familiar stories, and each episode in such stories lends itself to a human personal and psychological situation that can be given a meaning.

HERACLES (HERCULES)

HERACLES (HERCULES) = Any human facing and solving the problems of everyday living. Some of our problems and how we may solve them are illustrated here. Heracles was a son of Zeus and a human mother and had unusual physical strength and determination. His "Labours" can be equated with courses of study.

HERACLES = Glory of Hera = Glory of goddess = Glory of God = Glory of Life (Son of a god (Zeus)).

The Labours of Heracles may also be taken as representative of some of human life's problems. (As an actual person he did not exist. True of other mythical persons also).

The First Labour was one he chose himself, i.e. to kill the NEMEAN LION. It had to be killed by his bare hands, and because nothing could pierce its skin, he had to flay it with its own claws. He made use of its skin as protective armour.

This could be our graduation from school studies where we have to take full responsibility for the exams (ourselves only), and we can use the result or Diploma (lion's skin) as a qualification in the future.

The other labours were required to be done at the behest of Eurystheus his mentor.

The Second Labour was to slay the LERNEAN HYDRA with nine heads. It lived in a swamp. Any place with water apparently indicates an intellectual experience in this myth. As a head was cut off another grew in its place. But one head was immortal. His cousin Iolaus helped him by cauterizing the stump as each head was cut off. When the nine heads were cut off the animal died -- he thrust the immortal head under a large rock. He dipped his arrows in the poisonous blood so they were lethal in battle.

The water involved in the swamp suggests an intellectual problem, and the subject one with nine divisions. He needed help to conclude his studies of each division but the immortal head or division was his own responsibility -- possibly the exam to pass. The poison was the knowledge he could use to solve problems.

The Third Labour was to bring back alive a female deer (CERYINEINIAN HIND) from a mountainous area. It took him a year and its capture was made at the source of a river in the mountains. The goddess Artemis (of wildlife) rebuked him for the capture.

The elusive nature of this Labour indicates it may be an early form of science.

The Fourth Labour was to capture alive and bring back the EURYMANTHIAN BOAR a large and ferocious beast ("Eurymanthus" meant foretelling by casting lots, so the subject may have been akin to statistics). Bringing it back alive might mean it could then be used in other studies.

The Fifth Labour was to clean out the cattle STABLES OF AUGIEAS. They had not been cleaned for many years and was an enormous amount of manure. It was causing a lot of pollution in the area and harmful to people The stables had to be cleaned out in one day. With some help he turned the course of two rivers to run through the stables and washed all the dung away.

Apparently Augeias was a professor who did not revise his course for many years so it had become a lot of bull, and was no longer useful and really harmful to his students. The work of a lot of running water suggests an intellectual revision and discarding the unrevised subject matter. Augeias was not pleased.

The Sixth Labour was to drive away a countless flock of clawed birds from the STYMPHALIAN marsh. They were doing great harm to people poisoning the area with their manure. This was possibly gossip. He needed the advice of Athene (wisdom), so could then shoot them with his arrows. Cut down the gossip and possibly the gossipers.

The Seventh Labour was to capture the BULL RAVAGING CRETE. In a watered plain it was tearing up crops and battering down walls -- namely, creating violence in a school. After a long struggle he threw it down and tamed it, and brought it back alive. Then it was set free --- made into games.

The Eighth Labour was to capture the four man-eating MARES OF DIOMEDES, a professor who used his subject to fail students. Diomedes used his warriors to corner Heracles -- but he cut them off with an arm of the sea, and stunned Diomedes with his club. He then fed Diomedes to his mares -- overcame him with his own subject. He then harnessed the mares -- made the subject useful.

The Ninth Labour was to obtain the golden GIRDLE OF HIPPOLYTE, the queen of the Amazons. Hippolyte gave Heracles the girdle as a gift, but the goddess Hera stirred up trouble and there was a battle where many were killed including Hippolyte. Hera represents an authority not satisfied with easy success of a student.

The Tenth Labour was to bring back the RED CATTLE OF GERYON He had to kill Geryon and his helpers, but then herded the cattle over a long distance having many adventures on the way. This represented his teaching Geryon's subject for a long period.

The Eleventh Labour was to bring back three APPLES FROM THE GARDEN OF THE HESPERIDES (the daughters of the giant Atlas). He asked Atlas to get the apples for him. Atlas was carrying the sky on his shoulders -- he knew a lot about Astronomy. He offered to get the apples if Heracles

would hold the sky while he was gone. Heracles stood on
a nearby mountain and held the sky -- he knew
Astronomy as well as Atlas. When Atlas brought back the
apples, he was not in a hurry to take the sky again, but
Heracles asked him to take it while he adjusted his cloak
as a cushion, and he did so. Heracles then walked off
with the apples (he had assumed the duty of teaching
Astronomy for a short period only).   The apples were
later returned to the Hesperides.

      The Twelfth and final Labour was to bring up to
earth the three-headed dog, CERBERUS, the guard dog
from the gates of Tartarus, the Greek abode of the dead.
Hades agreed if he would use only his bare hands to
capture and bring the dog out to the daylight. He had
the help of Athene and Hermes but needed to have
instructions before proceeding. The dog had been
chained to the gates of Tartarus indicating the rigidity of
dogma. It feared the daylight, indicating that these
studies could not stand the "light of day" applied to
them.   These appear to have been religious studies.

THESEUS

THESEUS = Son of Poseidon God of the Sea) = Son of
(Neptune) = Son of a GOD = (intellectual) LIFE

      Theseus decided himself that when he became a
man he would perform Labours as his cousin Heracles
had done. With his mother's blessing he started on a
journey to Athens through countryside where he would

meet with many harmful things he would have to remedy. These are listed as follows (most of the men claimed to be "sons of Poseidon" = teachers).

PERIPHETES ("notorious": killed people with a bronze club). He taught Bronze Age skills. Theseus killed him but kept the bronze club, i.e. could make use of the skills in future.

PITYOCAMPTES ("pinebender"): he killed people by having them hold on to a pine he bent down to the ground. He then let go and they were flung to their deaths. He taught Forestry but failed his students. Theseus served him as he served his students -- making his subject attainable.

CROMMYUM SOW (monstrous sow destroying crops and harassing farmers). It attacked Theseus but he killed it with his club and gave a feast to the farmers. The subject was Agriculture but was being taught in a way not benefitting farmers.

SCIRON ("violent breeze"). He abducted travellers, forced them to wash his feet but then kicked them over a cliff into the sea where they were eaten by a giant turtle. He taught Hygiene. Theseus flung him over the cliff when he kicked. Obliged him to modify his course.

CERCYON ("boar"). He was exceptionally strong and invited people to wrestle with him, but crushed them to death. Theseus was skilled in wrestling, flung him on his head and broke his neck. His subject could have been Athletics. He had to allow his students success in his course.

PROCRUSTES ("stretcher-out"). Forced people to fit into a bed by stretching them or lopping off part of them to fit the bed. Tried to make his students fit into his subject rather than his subject to fit his students. Theseus taught him the difference.

THE MINOTAUR (Monster with head of bull and body of man). Offspring of the wife of MINOS of Crete and a white Bull given by Poseidon. Youths from Greece were given as war sacrifice to be killed and eaten by it periodically. Theseus volunteered to go with them. With the help of Ariadne, a daughter of Minos, he found the monster in a labyrinth and killed it. With the youths whose lives he had saved thereby, he returned on the vessel back to Greece. But he forgot to take down the black sail on the vessel they were sent in, and his father seeing it, thought his son had been destroyed, and in grief flung himself to his death into the sea.

This myth of Theseus shows how our sexual development when we are young does not have to be an uncontrollable monster, but a useful and pleasurable experience to us.   But it is important to remember to "take down the black sail" between us and our parents and others who can be helpful in such circumstances.

ARIADNE = HELPFUL. CARING

Ariadne was the daughter of Minos and Pasiphae of Crete.   She fell in love with Theseus and helped him find his way to the Minotaur in the labyrinth. Theseus promised to marry her but inadvertently left her on an island when on his way back to Athens with the young people he had saved from the Minotaur. She was rescued by Dionysus, the god of wine, fruit and vegetation in general, who married her.

LABYRINTH = COMPLEXITY, HIDING

Daedalus, a skilled craftsman, built the labyrinth, a complex maze, for King Minos of Crete, mainly to provide a hiding place for the Minotaur (man's body with bull's head) an offspring of Pasiphae, the wife of Minos, and a white bull. The event was initiated by Poseidon who had given the bull for sacrifice to himself, but Minos had substituted an inferior bull for the sacrifice and kept the white bull for himself.

TITAN = DOMINANCE, TYRANNY, RESISTANCE

The titans were giants who rebelled against the Olympic gods but were defeated by Zeus. They were possibly religious figures preceding the Olympic gods of classical Greece, but their religions were suppressed when the Olympic gods were introduced. They basically represented the strength of nature against human encroachments on the environment.

CADMUS = (FROM THE EAST) THOUGHTFUL

The Greek myth about Cadmus tells also about the struggle between religions and knowledge and reasoning in ancient Greece. This is shown in the story of the conflict between the Olympian gods and the Titans and Giants. The gods needed the help of a human (Heracles) to defeat them.

OLYMPIAN GODS' CONFLICT = STRUGGLE OF RELIGION WITH REASONING AND KNOWLEDGE

The myth tells about the struggle of the Olympian gods with the Titans, from which they recovered only to be attacked by a race of Giants they could not defeat without the help of Heracles to finish them off. Gods or religions could not exist without the help and observance of humans.

TYPHON = A LIBRARY OR A LOT OF KNOWLEDGE

The myth paints Typhon as a huge monster created by Mother Earth in response to the defeat of the Titans and giants by the Olympian gods and Heracles. Its expanse was enormous and it had one hundred human heads and many long arms. The Olympians fled from it, but Zeus, the chief god, tried to fight it. Zeus was beaten and all his sinews were taken out and he was left helpless in a cave.

CADMUS PLAYING A LUTE = CREATIVE HUMAN BEING, INDUSTRIUS

Typhon, hearing music, approaches the human and listens appreciatively as if it were a god understanding human activities and needs.

Cadmus, realizing the danger and aware that Zeus is in trouble, pretends his instrument needs repairs with new strings. Typhon gives him the sinews of Zeus. Cadmus leaves them where Zeus can get them.

This, in effect,   shows how humans often choose religious ideas rather than basic knowledge or reality.

ZEUS DEFEATING TYPHON = RELIGION BEING FAVOURED BY HUMANS

Zeus replacing his sinews, renewed his strength and his battle with Typhon using his thunderbolts to defeat him and confine him in the volcano of Aetna. This is illustrative of some people giving adherence to religious ideas rather than knowledge and reasoning. This has contributed to the existence of various religions.

CADMUS KILLING THE SERPENT = ACQUIRING KNOWLEDGE, STUDY

Zeus had promised Cadmus a reward for helping him defeat Typhon. This was to take the form of a city and he would be the ruler and would marry and live prosperously there.

He was advised to follow a cow and where it lay down was the place for the city. With some companions he set about planning and building.   They wanted a source of water and found it nearby, but it was guarded by a huge serpent of the god Ares.   It killed some of his men and Cadmus overcame it. He was advised by Athene to sow the teeth of the serpent at the spot and it generated a swarm of warriors armed for battle.   He threw a rock and hit one of them initiating conflict among them until all were killed except five who then helped him to build the city.

SOWING THE TEETH OF THE SERPENT= MAKING USE OF LOCAL KNOWLEDGE

Because the serpent was owned by Ares, who required redress for losing it, the Olympians decreed that Cadmus would serve Ares for eight years. This period could be considered a time of study some of which would include military knowledge since Ares was the God of War. The serpent's teeth had produced warriors who killed themselves but some of them survived and helped Cadmus.

CADMUS BUILT AN ACROPOLIS AND MARRIED HARMONIA = DEVELOPED A PERSONAL PHILOSOPHY MAKING USE OF HIS INTUITION

Cadmus and Harmonia lived a good life among his people and, finally retiring, found solace in the "happy isles of the west". We owe it to ourselves to know when to retire or change work for some recreative pursuit.

ODYSSEUS (ULYSSES)

ODYSSEUS = (ANGRY ONE) HUMAN AGAINST ADDICTION

The myth about Odysseus (Ulysses) and his trip back from Troy is possibly an account of anyone's "guilt trip". He had plenty of reason to feel guilty since he had accused falsely one of his countrymen (planted false but incriminating evidence) who for that reason was executed. Odysseus was noted for deceiving and telling lies.   Actually he may have made the journey alone, visiting various islands with his own agenda.

Told by himself, his adventures during his journey homeward are as follows: (essentially the stories are likely to be untruths)

RAID ON DEFENSELESS CITY OF ISMARUS =
TAKING GUILT OUT ON   SOMEONE INNOCENT

This resulted in loss of some of his men, or loss of his credibility.   They had obtained a lot of wine, got drunk and were kicked out.

LAND OF THE LOTUS EATERS = GIVING WAY TO
AN ADDICTION

Guilt sometimes leads to giving way to an addiction.   The lotus eaters gave the lotus to Odysseus' men resulting in their complete forgetfulness of their homes and where they were going.   Odysseus had to drag them to their ships and force them to leave.

CAPTURED IN THE CAVE OF POLYPHEMUS =
ATTEMPTED SUICIDE OR GIVING WAY TO A DEATH WISH

He is almost eaten with several of his men by the giant, Polyphemus, whom he injures by burning out his eye and then taunts and is cursed by him.   This incurred the wrath of Poseidon,   the god of the sea,   because the Cyclops were his creation.   The curse was that he should suffer shipwreck, lose all his men and arrive home alone to a lot of trouble.   The loss of men in the myth may be lies since he may have had none to begin with.

AEOLUS' GIFT OF BAD WINDS RELEASED BY HIS MEN = FRIENDS DO NOT HELP SOMEONE ADDICTED

He gave way to exhaustion after nine days awake steering his ship , and his men released the winds from the bag given him by Aeolus thinking it was treasure, so they were swept back to where they had to struggle again, rowing in a calm sea to reach home. Explaining to his men why the bag of winds should not be opened would have been common sense wisdom. However, it was a good excuse for not arriving home sooner.

Trying to go straight, however, in this instance, may be foiled by friends even though unintentionally.

LAND OF THE LASTRYGONES AND LOSS OF ELEVEN OF TWELVE SHIPS AND THEIR CREWS = GIVING IN AFTER A TEMPORARY SUCCESS IS A DISASTER

Loss of most of his men to cannibals is loss of much of his faculties consumed by his addiction. In the story his men brought their ships into a long narrow harbour, thinking they would be treated well by the inhabitants. Instead their ships were wrecked by them, and they then cannibalized the sailors. Odysseus had left his own ship outside the harbour, so he could escape from this disaster. A great loss and a narrow escape. Also an excuse for having so few men to accompany him during the rest of his journey.

ISLAND OF THE ENCHANTRESS CIRCE =
ATTEMPT AT RECOVERY

Intuitively he becomes aware there is more to life lived normally, and that humans can be human-like as well as animal-like in the way they live.

Circe welcomed his men but by enchantment changed them all into pigs. She had changed other visitors into animals also, and thought she could change Odysseus into a fox, but she was foiled by him through the help of the god Hermes. He then forced her to change all the men back into their natural state and give them her hospitality for many years. This was a cover story for his long relationship with Circe.

TRIP TO TARTARUS, THE PLACE OF DEATH =
ANOTHER DEATH WISH OR NEAR SUICIDE

He has to fight off old ideas of self-destruction, but tries to look forward to a better future. He wished to consult with a seer who had already died and gone to the Elysian fields. The seer told him what his future would be on his journey home and what awaited him there.

TIED TO THE MAST TO HEAR THE SONGS OF THE SIRENS BUT NEAR TO SYLLA AND CHARYBDIS = FOILED IN HIS EFFORTS TO ESCAPE ADDICTION AND PERSONAL DEPRESSION

He needs help but he insists on having the experience and there is more loss to the monsters of his addiction. He had put wax in the ears of his men so they couldn't hear the songs of the Sirens, and had told them to make sure he remained tied up. Hearing the songs could have led to his death by trying to go to the Sirens. But his men tied him more securely so he couldn't get free to destroy himself. Help of others can be a life saving experience.

LAND OF HYPERION'S FORBIDDEN CATTLE BUT HIS MEN KILL SOME = ANOTHER ATTEMPT TO GO STRAIGHT FOILED BY HIS FRIENDS

Because his men had killed some of the forbidden cattle, Poseidon punished them with a storm. As a result he lost the last of his men in the ensuing shipwreck and was himself drawn to Charybdis and almost drawn down (was in despair at his lack of success in overcoming his addiction).

DRIFTING TO THE ISLE OF BEAUTIFUL CALYPSO WHO LOVES HIM AND OFFERS HIM IMMORTALITY = FINAL RELIEF ON HIS OWN HELPED BY HIS INTUITION TO DO SOMETHING INTELLECTUAL SUCH AS WRITING A BOOK

All the story of struggling with the sea and the god Poseidon toward the end of his adventures indicates his achieving some mental control of his situation, and a break with his overwhelming addiction and suicide inclinations.

Clinging to the wreckage of his ship he drifted aimlessly but reached the island of Calypso who welcomed him and offered him immortality if he would stay with her. She was a death goddess. The immortality promised could mean producing writings that would have lasting value after his decease. He stayed with her seven years.

HIS LONGING FOR HOME AND FINAL STRUGGLE WITH THE SEA HELPED BY THE GODDESSES LEUCOTHEA AND ATHENE = WANTING A NORMAL LIFE AND ACCEPTING INTELLECTUAL HELP

This could mean his doing a course of study as a guide to his future work.

He embarked on a boat given him by Calypso but Poseidon became aware of his attempt and again made his transport a wreck and he was thrown into the sea. He was a good swimmer and managed to cling to some of the wreckage. Leucothea came to comfort him alighting on the wreckage as a sea mew, and Athene also realized that Poseidon finally had had enough punishing him, so she made sure he was able to reach the next island.

HIS LANDING ON THE ISLAND OF THE SHINING ONES, THE PHAEACIANS = HIS SUCCESS WITH THE COURSE AND POSSIBLY ITS EXAM

His reaching home at last is a personal success through accepting help and overcoming misfortune.

The rulers of the island treated him hospitably and provided him with a crew who brought him to Ithaca, his home. Poseidon wrecked the crew as they were returning to their island in vengeance for their helping Odysseus.

ELIMINATING THE SUITORS TO HIS WIFE PENELOPE = MEETING AND SOLVING THE PROBLEMS OF ORDINARY LIFE. TELLING MORE LIES (TO HIS WFE PENELOPE)

Settling down to routines of ordinary life is an accomplishment after his adventures. Odysseus met the suitors dressed as a wandering beggar and they abused him. However, his wife, Penelope, had given the suitors a contest using his bow to shoot an arrow through twelve rings. They were not strong enough even to bend the bow to string it, and when Odysseus had strung it and won the contest, he proceeded to shoot them with his arrows for their arrogance and misuse of his estate. He also had the women servants all killed because they had served the suitors.

The lies of Odysseus hoodwink most people into thinking this is a sequel to his journey. It is part of the myth and represent his boasting to Penelope about the men he had killed, and about the women he had met and not had relationships with (more lies)

CYCLOPS = ONE-SIDED, LACK OF REASONING

The Cyclops were one-eyed giants (with eye in forehead) created by Poseidon. They lived in caves and were mainly shepherds, but they also were workers of metals for the gods of Olympus. They were apparently cannibals when they had the opportunity, and were fierce and merciless in their contacts with humans. Seeing only one side of an issue can be defeatist.

CALYPSO = ACCEPTING DEFEAT, FORGETTING

Calypso was the daughter of the sea goddess Thetis and Oceanus. She was basically a death-goddess living alone in a great cavern surrounded by alders. Her parsley was an emblem of mourning and her iris a death flower. She persuaded Odysseus to stay with her for seven years, but he did not want heroic immortality as much as continuing life at his home, and finally recognized his longing. The gods Zeus and Hermes persuaded Calypso to let him go.

HESPERIDES = INSPIRATION, FRUITFULNESS

The Hesperides were the daughters of the Titan, Atlas, and were the keepers of a garden of Hera, the chief goddess of Olympus. They released the golden apples to Atlas for Heracles (oranges became available at an early time in Greece), but they were later returned to the garden. Heracles had to shoot Ladon, the serpent guarding the apple tree, but Hera sorrowing for him set him in the stars.

LAUREL = HIDDEN KNOWLEDGE, IMMORTALITY

The laurel was sacred to Apollo and indicated honour achieved in victory, so was used to crown the heroes. Also it was used to honour (crown) geniuses and wise persons whose contributions were immortal or wide-ranging in scope.

PROMETHEUS = FORETHOUGHT, INDEPENDENCE

Prometheus was a Titan and noted for his having helped humans by stealing fire from the gods for human use. For this he was punished by Zeus -- chained to a rock in the Caucasus with a vulture eating from his immortal liver. He was rescued from this torture by Heracles. He represents enterprise and independence, not caring about consequences. His bringing fire to humans may rather indicate the introduction of the arts and crafts to humans in early Greece.

EPIMETHEUS = AFTERTHOUGHT, CASUALNESS

Epimetheus was the brother of the titans Prometheus and Atlas. He was fearful of Zeus and other gods and ready to do anything to avoid or displease them. When Pandora was brought to him he accepted her as a gift without question and married her. But the gift was meant to be to his disadvantage. He represents fearfulness and lack of good sense and caring.

PANDORA = IRRESPONSIBILITY, UNWITTING ACTION

Pandora was the beautiful woman built by Hephaestus (Vulcan) at the request of Zeus. Zeus gave her to Epimetheus knowing what she would do. She was meant to bring unrequited longing and mischief to humans, and did so unthinkingly by opening a box of evils. She represents irresponsibility and an uncaring lack of control of events.

EOS = DAWNING, SEDUCING

Eos was the Dawn-maiden, daughter of the Titans Hyperion and Theia, and sister of Helius who conducted the sun across the heavens in his horse-drawn chariot every day. She was attracted to young male humans.

ORION = SKILLFUL HUNTER

Orion was the son of Poseidon and Euryale and the handsomest man alive. He fell in love with Merope a daughter of Oenopion, son of Dionysus, who promised him Merope in marriage if he would rid the island of Chios of dangerous beasts. This he accomplished, but Oenopion reneged on his promise. Disgusted, Orion drank much wine and went to bed with Merope. While he slept Oenopion put out both his eyes. He heard his eyesight could be restored by Helius in the far west, went there and this was done. He returned to Chios to have revenge on Oenopion who remained hidden, so he joined Artemis who shared his love of hunting. But he boasted he would rid the earth of all dangerous beasts. Apollo heard the boast and arranged for a monstrous scorpion to chase him. It could not be killed by a mortal weapon. While he swam in the sea, Apollo pretended to Artemis the swimmer was a dangerous person, and she shot and killed him with her unerring arrow. In great sorrow Artemis set his image and that of his dog in the stars where he is still pursued by the scorpion.

DEUCALION = SURVIVOR

Zeus in disgust at crimes of cannibalism committed by Lycaon and his sons, sent a flood to wipe out all humans.   Deucalion had been warned by Prometheus, his father, of this possibility, built an ark, loaded it with provisions and he and his wife Pyrrha went aboard.   It floated on the ensuing flood for nine days and, as the waters subsided, it stranded on Mount Parnassus. Deucalion sent out a dove and it did not return, so he and his wife disembarked and sacrificed to Zeus. They pleaded that humans be restored and their wish was granted.   They were told to take the bones of their mother -- rocks from Mother Earth -- and those thrown over their shoulders would become humans -- men as thrown by Deucalion and women as thrown by his wife.

LEDA = MOTHERING

Zeus fell in love with Leda, wife of Tyndareus, and coupled with her as a swan.   She as a consequence laid an egg which hatched out Helen (of Troy) and two sons Castor and Polydeuces (Pollux).   She was consequently deified as the goddess Nemesis.

NARCISSUS = SELF-LOVING

Narcissus was a handsome youth who repulsed young nymphs who loved him. For this reason the goddess Artemis condemned him to love someone who would not return his love.   This turned out to be his own image mirrored in a still pool of water. He pined away in frustration.

CALLISTO = CAPTIVATING

Callisto, a beautiful young woman, incurred the hatred and jealousy of Hera, the goddess wife of Zeus who had fallen love with her. Hera turned her into a bear. As a bear, she met her son who was out hunting. He was about to kill her when Zeus saw what was about to happen, and put them both in the stars as the Great and Little Bear near the Pole Star, Polaris.

JASON

JASON AND THE GOLDEN FLEECE = HUMAN ENDEAVOUR

Jason was encouraged by his uncle, King Pelias, to bring back the fleece of a sheep taken by his cousin Phrixus to the far distant country of Colchis.

Jason was the rightful heir to the throne usurped by his uncle who tried to get rid of him by promising him the throne if he would first go to Colchis and bring the golden fleece back to its final resting place. Pelias had killed his own brother Aeson and wife in order to reign as king.

THE ARGO AND ARGONAUTS = PHYSICAL AND MENTAL ATTRIBUTES OF A HUMAN

Organizing the building of a ship and manning it with heroes is personal development such as through a comprehensive education.

Jason was able to persuade many of the heroes of his country to embark on an adventure which would bring them honour as well as giving rest to the deceased prince of their country, Phrixus.

BRINGING BACK THE GOLDEN FLEECE = A GOAL IN LIFE

The sense of a great adventure was attractive to Jason as well as the heroes he asked to accompany him. The gods of Olympus were also in favour and assisted in various ways, including the building of the Argo.

KING AIETES' ANGER AND BITTERNESS = HOSTILITY, INHOSPITABLE

Aietes was not happy with strangers coming into his country with their demands for an article he had already established as a momento, and had guarded by a huge serpent in a sacred grove. He had demanded they leave his country when he met them, but was persuaded mainly by his daughter, Medea, that they be accommodated in their quest. He declared they must first undergo tests and if they failed would lose their lives.

MEDEA = SORCERY, POWER OF INTUITION AND KNOWLEDGE

In mythology women often represent intuition and intelligence.

Medea was a sorceress with considerable powers in the black arts. She was feared by her father who threatened to kill her if she helped Jason and the Argonauts. She was reputed to have a magic chariot drawn by dragons and in which she could be airborne to travel great distances. She gave Jason a magic ointment conferring invincibility for one day. This enabled him to succeed in the tests set by Aietes.

FIRE-BREATHING BULLS = PASSIONS, HATES, ETC., HINDERING PLANS OF OPERATION

Jason was able to tame the bulls and yoke them to a plow although they resisted vigorously, breathing fire.

Self-control is essential to any successful operation.

PLOWING THE SACRED FIELD = WORKING ENTHUSIASM

To the surprise of Aietes and his warriors Jason succeeded in plowing the field of the god Ares with the brazen bulls. Aietes suspected his daughter Medea for giving the essential help to Jason without which he could not have succeeded. Jason demonstrated his readiness.

SOWING THE DRAGON'S TEETH = PRESENTING IDEAS OF ACTION

This is a sowing of some of the dragon's teeth still available from those used by Cadmus. The teeth were sowed in the plowed drills in the field. Strong ideas.

ARMED WARRIORS ARISING = CONFLICTING ARGUMENTS

The teeth "germinated", each one producing an armed warrior rising from the soil. They were ready for combat and advanced on Jason. These were arguments used against Jason in the debate,

HITTING WARRIOR WITH HELMET = PRESENTING GOOD REASONING

Jason had been instructed by Medea to throw his helmet to hit one of the sown warriors who would then attack each other, blaming his fellow for attack. Using something from his head suggests it was an argument Jason thought of and used to advantage.

WARRIORS DESTROY THEMSELVES = REASONING IS EFFECTIVE

The warriors fought among themselves until only a few were left. These attacked Jason but he was able to finish them off with his weapons. They could not hurt him because he had used the ointment given him by Medea. Arguments used against Jason were ineffective.

APPROACHING THE GROVE AT NIGHT WITH MEDEA = SLEEPING ON IDEA FOR ACTION

Medea instructed Jason to not lose time but to proceed the same night of the contest to the sacred grove where the golden fleece was kept guarded by a dragon.

SACRIFICING TO BRIMO (GODDESS CERES) = PRAYING FOR SUCCESS

Brimo, a witch-huntress, was the owner and guardian of the sacred grove. They had to sacrifice a lamb to her. When she had come, eaten the gore and departed, the gates to the grove opened and they could enter. The glow of the fleece lighted their way.

CALMING THE GUARDIAN DRAGON = CONTROL OF THE SITUATION

As they approached the dragon it uttered a deep roar that rocked the forest and the town, but it quieted at the touch of Medea. Orpheus played his music of sleep and relaxation and the dragon settled down.

TAKING THE GOLDEN FLEECE = REALIZING THE OBJECTIVE

Jason hastily took the fleece from where it was hung and they left the grove as quickly as possible. They hurried to the Argo in which they set sail at once heading for home. Medea left with Jason for fear of her father's threats and on promise of wedding Jason. She also persuaded her young brother to accompany them, but murdered him, and threw his body parts into the sea to delay his father who was pursuing them.

MUSIC OF ORPHEUS = REALIZING IMPORTANCE OF THE ARTS IN HUMAN LIFE

Since this is basically a journey through life, the contribution of Orpheus, the master musician, was essential to their success since it calmed the dragon, permitting their escape from the guarded grove. When required, the influence of music in human life has always been considerable. The arts are an essential part of human enjoyment and creativity.

TAKING THE FLEECE HOME = APPLYING WHAT HAS BEEN LEARNED

Achieving the objective of the journey is a success in life, repeated many times as human endeavour is applied to what challenges occur and human knowledge can effect. It is unfortunate that some successes are achieved through crime (Medea murdering her brother),

but the future results are often compensatory. Medea eventually loses out and has to flee back to Colchis.

PELIAS = URSURPER, SELFISHNESS

Pelias was Jason's uncle who had usurped the throne of Aeson, Jason's father, and later murdered Aeson and his wife Polymele. He had persuaded Jason to bring back the golden fleece from Colchis in order to get rid of him. When Jason returned Pelias had promised to surrender the throne to him. This he was not inclined to do. However, on the pretext of his rejuvenation by magic, Medea, as Jason's wife, tricked his daughters into cutting him into pieces, hoping to restore his youth. Medea then left in her aerial car drawn by dragons.

AGAMEMNON = LEADING, RISK TAKING

Agamemnon was the chief king of Mycenae and the leader of the Greek forces setting out to punish Paris of Troy who had persuaded Helen, the wife of Menelaus, to leave her husband and live with him at Troy. The Greek princes had sworn to aid the one who married Helen if any conflict occurred as a consequence. When he returned victorious from Troy, his wife and her lover treacherously murdered him.

MENELAUS = DECEIVED, WRONGED

Menelaus, the king of Sparta and husband of Helen, was helped by his brother, Agamemnon, and leaders of the Greek states to destroy Troy and bring back Helen to Sparta.

HELEN = DECEIVING, IRRESPONSIBILE

Helen was reputed to be the most beautiful woman in the world (Greece). She was a daughter of Zeus, chief Olympic god, and a human. She was basically a goddess because of her birth and finally was taken to Olympus. Paris (Androclos) of Troy had judged Aphrodite to be the most beautiful of the three goddesses (Hera, Athene and Aphrodite) in consideration of his winning the most beautiful woman in the world, Helen. The unusual myth of her birth was that she had been hatched from an egg. Zeus had assumed the form of a swan when he had become her father.

CLYTAEMNESTRA = FAITHLESS, TREACHEROUS

Clytaemnestra, the wife of Agamemnon, had been persuaded into a relationship with Aegisthus, while her husband was engaged in the battle for Troy. Both of them planned to kill Agamemnon when he returned. He was persuaded to take a bath before a feast for his homecoming, and while he was doing so, his wife threw a net over him and he was helpless to being killed with a sword thrust by Aegisthus.

CASSANDRA = FORETELLING

Cassandra was a prophetess of Troy. She was given to Agamemnon as part of the spoils of war in the destruction of Troy by the Greeks, and had two children for him. But she and her children were murdered by Agamemnon's wife when he was killed by her and her lover. She had been taught by Apollo, but when she resisted his advances, he removed her ability to convince anyone of the authenticity of her prophecies.

ELECTRA = VENGENCE, DUTIFULNESS

Electra, a daughter of Agamemnon, was determined to avenge the death of her father by her mother Clytaemnestra and her lover Aegisthus. She kept reminding her brother, Orestes, of his duty to kill them both for their deed, and was glad when he returned to Sparta and accomplished this.

IPHIGENIA = COOPERATIVE

Iphigenia was also a daughter of Agamemnon. When contrary winds prevented the Greek ships from sailing to Troy, Agamemnon was forced to allow her to be sacrificed to the goddess of wildlife, Artemis, who had caused the difficulty. She consented but when the ritual was about to be done, Artemis took her away to be one of her priestesses. She later helped her brother, Orestes, to escape from the Taurians.

TROY = CONTROVERSY, PROBLEMATIC SITUATION

Troy appears to have been a problem to be solved in various ways. It is portrayed as a walled city built by Poseidon and Apollo (Apollo played music while Poseidon was building it). Poseidon, god of the sea and intellectual activity, acted against the Trojans in the siege by the Greeks; Apollo worked for the Trojans. Stories of Troy indicate it was razed by Heracles and 300 men when Priam, the king, refused to give him the immortal horses he had won in a fair contest. In the struggle between Hector and Achilles they ran around the city three times before Hector was killed, indicating it could not have been very big, or suggesting it was something other than a city. It could have been an argument.

ACHILLES = STRENGTH OF PURPOSE, DETERMINATION

Achilles was the greatest warrior in the Greek forces attacking Troy in the Iliad or Homer's story of Troy. He had not wanted to go with the army but had been persuaded. He was destined to kill the great warrior of Troy, Hector, but to also lose his life in the struggle for the destruction of Troy.

HECTOR = SUPPORTER, DUTIFUL

Hector was the chief warrior in the defense of Troy against the Greeks. He was one of the sons of the king of Troy, Priam, and led the defense of the city as his duty, although he knew he was fated to not survive the conflict. Achilles was his chief enemy but he waged successful war

against many of the heroes of the Greek army.   In the
end the gods failed to give him their support and he fell
to the onslaught of Achilles.

PARIS (ANDROCLES) = HUMANNESS, WEAKNESS

Paris was a shepherd, but he was chosen to decide
which of the goddesses was the most beautiful (through
the machinations of Eris, the goddess of strife) of Hera,
Athene and Aphrodite. All were beautiful but what they
promised conditioned his decision. Aphrodite promised
him love of the most beautiful woman in the world so he
decided in her favour. The anger and disappointment of
the other goddesses, particularly of Hera, led to the war
against Troy, his home. The overt reason was his
taking of Helen, the wife of Menelaus (a Greek king),
to be his lover at Troy.

WOODEN HORSE = TRICKERY

The Greeks built a wooden horse on the advice of
Athene (claimed by Odysseus) to hold in its hollow body
a number of men who would open the gates of Troy when
the horse was inside the city.   They left one of their men
to convince the Trojans to take the horse into the city. It
was a successful ruse, although Cassandra and Lacoon
foresaw what would happen and told the Trojans the
horse carried Greek warriors. They were not believed.
Odysseus was in the horse and kept the men quiet until it
was time to get out and open the gates to the returning
Greek army. The army entered the city and destroyed
its inhabitants.

LAOCOON = PERCEPTIVE, PROPHETIC

Laocoön, a Trojan priest of Apollo, recognized the wooden horse as a ruse of Odysseus, and advised Priam to destroy it. He had, however, fallen out of favour with Apollo who now refused his sacrifice to Poseidon and sent two serpents to destroy him. The serpents first killed his twin sons and then killed him. The Trojans thought this was a sign he was in the wrong to condemn the horse being brought into Troy. Cassandra had told the Trojans the horse had men inside it, too, but, as usual, she was not believed.

PATROCLUS = FRIENDSHIP

Patroclus was the best friend of Achilles. When Achilles withdrew from the conflict because of his quarrel with Agamemnon, the Trojans had considerable success against the Greeks and even set fire to some of the Greek ships. Patroclus saw the danger and persuaded Achilles to let him wear his armour and enter the fray. The Trojans thought he was Achilles and many ran for shelter, and he was able to turn the tide for a while. But Apollo recognized his deception and hit him a severe blow and tore the armour from him. Thus exposed he was easy prey to a Trojan and was finished off by Hector. Achilles was devastated by the death of his best friend and re-entered the battle.

AENEAS = PRAISWORTHY

Aeneas was the son of Aphrodite, the goddess of love, and a human, Anchises, a cousin of Priam. He took part in the defense of Troy and proved himself in battle. But he was favoured by the gods who helped him when in difficult situations against Achilles, for example. When Troy fell he and many of his followers escaped and sailed away to the west where he was destined to form the basis of the Roman Empire.

TURNUS = JEALOUS, COMBATIVE

Turnus was a rival of Aeneas for the hand of Lavinia the heir to the kingdom of Latium. When Aeneas arrived at Latium with his Trojans he was recognized by Latinus, the king, to be a prospective bridegroom for the princess, Lavinia, his daughter, because he had been told in a dream she should marry a person from a distant country. Turnus, was opposed to this idea and as the leader of an army of Rutulians, determined to destroy Aeneas and the Trojans accompanying him, to make way for his own suit for Lavinia. During the conflict he was finally slain by Aeneas.

CAMILLA = GALLANTRY

Camilla was the leader of a cavalry of women warriors. She led the Volscians against Aeneas and the Trojans in support of Turnus. She was killed by a Trojan hunter and then taken to her refuge by the goddess Diana (Artemis). Her leaderless cavalry left the field of combat.

MEZENTIUS = HATEFUL, CRUEL

Mezentius had incurred the hatred of the Etruscans because of his cruelty and had been driven out of their country. He was assisting Turnus and the Rutulians in their fight against Aeneas and the Trojans when he was killed by Aeneas.

PALLAS = DUTIFUL, YOUTHFUL

Pallas was the son and heir of Evander, king of the Arcadians, who agreed to help Aeneas against Turnus and the Rutulians, opposing the Trojans. Pallas was young and inexperienced in battle and was killed by Turnus.

LAVINIA = PROSPECTIVE BRIDE

Lavinia was the daughter of Latinus, king of Latium, where Aeneas and his Trojans landed after their flight from Troy, and where Aeneas planned to settle with his followers and build a nation. It had been foretold Lavinia would marry a person from a foreign country and Aeneas appeared to be the one. After the Trojans were successful against the opposing armies led by Turnus they were allowed to build a city and Aeneas married Lavinia.

ABRAHAM =FAITHFUL

Returning to the biblical myths -- ideas represented by persons, etc., as in the Greek myths, indicate complex symbols of human conditions.

"Abraham" seems to be representative of a way of life anyone could have under the guidance of a master plan. His plan or purpose needed his wife Sarah-- his intellectual and intuitive ability -- as well. His accomplishments would bring great and lasting value to very many people in perpetuity.

Some symbolic aspects of Abraham's progress are as follows.

A SACRIFICE of a heifer, a ram, a goat (all three-year old), and a dove and a pigeon had to be made, and all were placed on an altar. In a dream he saw a SMOKING FURNACE and a LIGHTED LAMP that moved among the items on the altar. The Sacrifice indicated a presentation of his plan to an authority. The number three in this writing refers to religious authority. The smoking furnace (not burning properly) refers to his questionable enthusiasm for the project; the lighted lamp a burning zeal to get it done.

As he gets the sacrifice ready, Abraham falls asleep and has a GREAT HORROR OF DARKNESS. He fears that he may not know enough to do what he has planned.

GOING TO EGYPT = improving on one's education.

GOING TO LIVE ON A PLAIN = Setting up a business where there is none already and therefore no competition. Abraham's nephew, Lot, who had accompanied him when he left Ur and when he went into Egypt, set up at the neighbouring plain of Sodom and Gomorrah.

DESTRUCTION BY FIRE AND BRIMSTONE FROM HEAVEN = BECOMING VERY ANGRY IN OVERCOMING AN ADDICTION TO A DESTRUCTIVE HABIT.

This seems to have been a problem for Lot who had been in conflict with some kings of the area, and was helped by Abraham. The "sins" associated with the plain could have also represented Lot's personal problem.

TURNING INTO A PILLAR OF SALT = Seeing in a crystal clear way that one must break with an old way of behaviour.

LIVING IN A CAVE IN A MOUNTAIN = Separating oneself from people or temptation to carry on in an old destructive habit, and succeeding in this way. Doing something with a high purpose.

DAUGHTERS HELPING ONE TO HAVE PROGENY = Your intuition to help you devise a productive plan for the future. (This part of the myth is assigned to Lot, Abraham's nephew, who is not mentioned afterwards).

ABRAHAM'S AT LAST HAVING A SON = FINALLY FINISHING OR PERFECTING A PROJECT

Abraham's wife, Sarah, gave birth to a son at ninety years of age, and they gave him the name of Isaac. Abraham was one hundred years of age. The ages represent a level of achievement according to number codes used in ancient times.

ESAU AND JACOB

ESAU = CHOICE OF PHYSICAL ACTIVITYAS A WAY OF LIVING (BASICALY "HUNTING AND GATHERING")

In the biblical story Esau chose to be a hunter gatherer, different in his more primitive way of living from Jacob, who chose to be an agriculturist, a shepherd and stock farmer.

JACOB = CHOICE OF MORE INTELLECTUAL ACTIVITY IN HIS WAY OF LIVING FROM THAT OF ESAU

JACOB

JACOB (a Supplanter) is apparently a very special representation of human life in its physical and intellectual characteristics.

That his name was changed to ISRAEL (a Prince) enforces this idea. Also his life was more oriented to intellectual pursuits than that of his brother Esau. They were non-identical twins.

The rejection of an ESAU type of person is determined at the beginning of the myth where he sells his birthright and is cheated out of his blessing.

Jacob leaving home to venture on his own is any person's way of becoming an individual.

JACOB'S LADDER shows his optimistic thoughts -- angels going upwards to heaven; and his pessimistic thoughts -- those coming down, were attitudes he would have to modify to his advantage.

WORKING TO WIN RACHEL FOR A WIFE is his studying to improve his reasoning ability (intellectual studies).

WINNING LEAH AS A WIFE is his attaining physical ability through work and training.

His physical characteristics were most important at the beginning of his career and they are represented by his sons and a daughter as follows:

REUBEN to be able to see what is needed to be seen.

SIMEON to hear and understand. Attentive.

LEVI to sense and feel. Intuitive.

JUDAH to have an understanding of odors. Physical sense.

ISSACHAR to develop physical strength. Athletic.

ZEBULUN to learn to find the way. Spatial sense.

DAN to be wise in judgement. Fairness.

GAD to learn to be a leader. Pioneering.

NAPHTHALI to learn to be a speaker. Orator.

ASHER to appreciate the Arts. Perceptible.

JOSEPH to have good commercial sense.

BENJAMIN to have a love of adventure. Adventurous.

DINAH to be able to make use of intuition and knowledge.

(Jacob discusses some of the attributes of his sons in Chapter 49 of the Book of Genesis in the Bible).

With these attributes a human being is able to make her/his way in life. It is time then to set out as a person dependent on oneself for making a living and even undertaking worthwhile projects to benefit humanity. To just live a sterile existence is not enough. One must attempt to continue to do something for society and the environment, and to improve oneself, such as getting more education if it is available. There is sometimes a disadvantage in this. Some education systems impose ideas too rigid and unmodifiable or not in the best interest of the student. It is always necessary to evaluate the strengths and deficiencies of the education systems.

MOSES = INDPENDANT HUMAN BEING

Like being left as a baby in an ark on a river of independence. But to accept help from a higher authority such as parents is necessary. Learning is part of experience and inevitable from the start, but a time may come when asserting a break is possible. Then you may have to spend some time shepherding your woolly ideas,   until you can find inspiration like a "burning bush" to spur you to do your lifeworthy project.

LET MY PEOPLE GO = LET ME BE FREE OF PREJUDICES

But first of all taking an inventory of the worthwhileness of your education may be appropriate. Looking at the failings or rigidity of the system you followed you may be able to see they are somewhat like PLAGUES.

1. ALL WATER TURNING INTO BLOOD MAKING FOUL SMELL =   CHEMISTRY.

The First Plague was the turning of all water in the land into blood . It caused great distress. Then the blood rotted causing foul smells.

2. MYRIADS OF FROGS WHICH DIE AND SMELL = BIOLOGY

The Second Plague was a countless number of frogs occurring all over the land. They all died and rotted causing a foul smell.

3. ALL DUST BECOME LICE = ROTE LEARNING OF ISOLATED FACTS

The Third Plague was lice, as many as all the dust in the land, a severe source of irritation to all people.

4. SWARMS OF FLIES EVERYWHERE = UNRELATED LITERAL IDEAS

The Fourth Plague was a swarm of flies in houses and everywhere.

5. DISEASE OF CATTLE KILLING THEM = VETERINARY SCIENCE

The Fifth Plague was a murrain or disease of cattle which killed all of them in the country.

6. ASHES BECOME BOILS ON PEOPLE = MEDICAL   STUDIES

The Sixth Plague was that ashes from their domestic fires became boils on all the people causing great distress.

7. HAIL AND LIGHTNING DESTROYNG = PHYSICS

The Seventh Plague was a storm of hail and lightning destroying crops and cattle.

8. SWARMS OF LOCUSTS = AGRICULTURAL SCIENCE

The Eighth Plague was an east wind that brought clouds of locusts destroying all vegetation in the country.

9. THREE DAYS OF DARKNESS = RELIGIOUS STUDIES

The Ninth Plague was three days of complete darkness throughout the land.

10. FIRSTBORN OF EVERY FAMILY KILLED. FIRSTBORN BEING OBLIGED TO BE EDUCATED SO THEY COULD NO LONGER THINK FOR THEMSELVES.

The Tenth Plague occasioned the death of every firstborn Egyptian child in the country. The oldest child was the one to be educated. Assessed as an educational fault, it could be that the education system resulted in persons not having an incentive to think for themselves after being "educated", so they might be considered as finished with thinking or dead.

Having examined the educational system and seen its weaknesses and how it had contributed to prejudices, he/she can now free the mind as much as possible and pass over to a clearer view of things. A life plan now becomes possible and it involves a new project, namely, to research and write a book of value to all humanity (a "promised land").

A SEA TO CROSS = A LIBRARY TO DO RESEARCH

The first step to be taken then is to do some research at a library, for example. A great mass of ideas to be examined is like a sea to cross. Such a sea opens up and all energies go into finding the important aspects of the research plan as much as possible until the "sea is crossed" -- as much as can be found is found. Any part of former education may still be of some influence but basically it can be left behind or (suppressed) covered up, like the sea closing over.

LIVING IN A DESERT = WITHOUT HELP OF REFERENCES OR HELP FROM OTHER PEOPLE

Writing such a book has to be an independent task. Getting ideas to come through independent thinking is like getting water from a rock or manna from heaven. Inspiration is most helpful and is like going into a mountain to communicate with god. Former influences such as those of religious thinking have to be suppressed. The book has to be free of prejudices as much as possible.

Taking care that what is written is not engraved in stone is a caution. "Written in stone" still reflects rigid thinking and indicates that some things may not be easy to change if necessary (it always is necessary). Breaking the tablets is a beginning.

But the book is finally written and it is "a portable fatherland, the Torah"(Liptzin, 1985) -- the "Promised Land". It is also the "Ark of the Covenant", a guide for anyone or everyone in future as well as for the Hebrews of ancient time. The first five books of the present Holy Bible contain the mythology of the ancient Hebrews.

Incidentally the addition of a lot of the history of the Hebrews to the Bible has led to its being considered a historical record throughout the book. But the first five books or sections are definitely mythological and not historical.

WALLS OF JERICHO FALL DOWN = PEOPLE ARE SHOWN THE BOOK

Men, women and children are shown the book -- it is taken around the city several times (by Joshua, the leader) and finally allowed to be seen by people of this and many places and made known to them, like "slaying" or convincing them.

THE SUN TO STAND STILL = TO BE GIVEN SUFFICIENT TIME

Joshua needed the extra time to get people who were resistant to seeing or buying the book to be able to show them what they were missing.

[Apparently the early books of the Bible were written during the 80 years (about 600 BC) while the Hebrews were in captivity in Babylon. Some of the earliest writings of the Sumerians and other peoples of the Middle East could have been available to them and the religious practices and early mythology of Creation, etc, would also be well known to them. With such knowledge as a basis for their own creativity the writing of an expression of their own religious ideas was possible. But when they were released to go back to their former lands after eighty years they must have been very different from the original captives.]

SOME ARABIC MYTHS

SINDBAD THE SAILOR = STUDENT

The myth of Sindbad the Sailor appears typical of a student's endeavours in getting an education. He tells the story himself like Odysseus did when telling of his voyage home from Troy.

VOYAGES AT SEA = COURSES OF STUDY (THE SEA IN MYTHS INDICATES INTELLECTUAL ACTIVITY)

Symbols from the voyages can be interpreted as events or parts of some courses of study of a particular student. In mythology events at sea or with water are apparently considered intellectual experiences.

First Voyage

ISLAND THAT SUBMERGES LEAVING PEOPLE STRUGGLING IN THE WATER = DISCONTINUED COURSE LEAVING STUDENTS WITHOUT INSTRUCTION

Sindbad and his shipmates are allowed ashore on a beautiful island but their activity causes the island (a large sea creature) to submerge, and all the men but Sindbad are drowned. This indicates discontinuation of a particular course of study.

REACHING NEW ISLAND = RENEWAL OF STUDY

By dint of swimming ability Sindbad reaches a real island and clambers ashore. There he meets men with a number of mares which they hope to mate with a "sea horse". When this is accomplished they drive the "sea horse" away and return to their homes.

MARES NEEDING SERVICE = FACTUAL MATERIAL TO STUDY

Apparently this represents study material needing revision. When the revision is done the course can continue or another term can be undertaken. Sindbad took advantage of help to return to his home.

Second Voyage

ASLEEP ON DESERT ISLAND = NOT KNOWING WHAT COURSE TO TAKE

The ship arrives at an interesting island and the crew is allowed to go ashore for a rest. Sindbad, enjoying the climate, lies down for a rest and falls asleep. To his dismay when he awakes he finds the ship has gone and left him stranded. He apparently had not been admitted to the course of study he had expected.

LARGE EGG OF ROKH = NEW COURSE

Sindbad set out to explore the island to see if there were a possibility of escape and spied a large white object far off. As he approached it the sky was suddenly darkened by an immense bird which arrived to sit on the egg. It was a Rokh. Compared to it, Sindbad is very small. To escape the island he contrived to tie himself to one of the legs of the rokh hoping it would carry him to some other place such as the mainland. He thought the course was too advanced for him.

ROKH (IMMENSE BIRD) = TEACHER

Since the story is about studies, it is possible the Rokh represents a learned professor.

TYING HIMSLF TO LEG OF THE ROKH = ACCEPTING SERVICE OF TEACHER

Sindbad embarked tentatively on studies with the professor.

LANDING IN VALLEY OF DIAMONDS = PRESENTING OF BRILLIANT IDEAS IN COURSE OF STUDY

When the rokh eventually took off, it flew to a place where it used to feed on serpents (the professor did studies himself) but it was also a valley of diamonds, a place where advanced studies could be done. Sindbad was afraid of the serpents (the studies were too advanced for him) and hid in a cave at night for protection.   He did not attempt to delve into the advanced material.

COLLECTING DIAMONDS = LEARNING FACTS IN COURSE

Sindbad saw the value of the diamonds and collected some of the best ones (brilliant ideas) he could find. He probably read the books.

MEAT DIAMONDS STICK TO = TECHNIQUE USED BY OTHER STUDENTS

Sindbad was surprised to see chunks of meat being thrown down from the steep cliffs into the valley, and saw this was a method of collecting the diamonds which became embedded in the meat. He saw also the meat was taken up to their nests by eagles foraging in the valley. Basically this was a technique of study used by other students to obtain the ideas in the course. Distant education?!

USING MEAT TO ESCAPE VALLEY = USING OTHER STUDENTS' TECHNIQUE

Sindbad saw a way to escape the valley if he tied himself to a chunk of meat and a large eagle would carry him to the top of the cliffs. He wanted to get out of the course.

MOLLIFYING MERCHANTS = APOLOGIZING TO STUDENTS BY SHARING IDEAS

When the merchants (students) found him in an eagle's nest, they were annoyed he had make use of their method to escape the valley. He was encroaching. But he offered them some of the diamonds he had collected

-- much better than those they usually found embedded in meat -- so they were mollified. They helped him reach home.   Student were pleased to access ideas they had not had before.

Third Voyage

STORM AND DREADED ISLAND =   CONFUSION ABOUT NEW COURSE

On Sindbad's next voyage his ship encountered a great storm and they were driven off course and took shelter at an island everybody feared because of its inhabitants.   Material in this course was known not to be suitable. Also the course was one nobody wanted to take.

SWARMING RED DWARFS = CONFUSING SUBJECT MATTER

The ship was boarded by a swarm of red dwarfs who dragged the ship ashore and forced everybody to go to another nearby island where they saw piles of human bones and roasting spits.   They were required to live in an oversized palace where their fears were exacerbated by meeting a one-eyed giant.   This monster seized one of their number and killed, roasted and ate him.   The professor was known to fail students and they feared him.

ONE-EYED MONSTER =   RIGIDITY IN ONE WAY ONLY OF SEEING THINGS

A one-eyed monster represents a teacher with a one-sided or prejudiced way of looking at things, not a

good course or method of teaching . Sindbad saw the
danger to himself and the other students (crew) and
planned how they could get out of this mess.

PUTTING OUT THE EYE OF THE MONSTER =
CONFRONTATION

Sindbad's plan was to heat one of the roasting spits
and when the monster was asleep they would burn out
his eye, depriving him of the ability to capture them.
Also he persuaded the crew to get wood and build rafts
they would use to escape the island. They succeeded in
blinding the giant and embarked on their rafts.   The
students abandoned the course to the outrage felt by the
teacher.

MONSTERS SINKING RAFTS WITH BOULDERS =
OPPOSITION OF TEACHERS AND PUBLIC
OPINION

Relatives of the blinded giant suddenly came to
his cries and proceeded to throw rocks at the rafts until
they had sunk all and drowned their occupants except the
one Sindbad and his two companions were on.   They
hurriedly propelled their raft out of reach and proceeded
to another island nearby where they landed in exhaustion.
Namely, the students were expelled from the course and
prevented from doing further studies.

SERPENTS EATING COMPANIONS =
PARADIGMS THAT FAIL FELLOW STUDENTS

Arriving at this new island (course) they were
confronted by serpents who seized and ate one of

Sindbad's companions (he failed the course).   Sindbad
and the other companion for fear of the serpents climbed
into a tree to sleep when night came, but the serpent
came again and seized the second companion and ate
him also (he failed the course too).   Sindbad built a
barricade around the tree for the second night foiling an
attack of the serpent (wrote the exam).   But in
desperation the next morning he went to the shore to
drown himself in the sea (wished to abandon the course).
However he spied a ship and waving his turban a boat
was launched to rescue him and he eventually reached
home.

A RESCUING SHIP = HELP FROM SOCIETY

The rescue represents help we may receive from
the society we live in even if we are not successful.

Fourth Voyage

HURRICAINE DESTROYING SHIP = EVENTS CANCELLING   COURSE

On his next voyage Sindbad's ship was overtaken
by a hurricane which wrecked it and he and some of his
companions made it to shore on a plank.   Most students
were expelled from this course or could not take it.

CANNIBALS OFFERING HERBS = DRUG DEALERS AND STUDENTS

When Sindbad and his companions reached shore
they were met by the inhabitants who offered them food
and a herb to eat.   Sindbad was suspicious of the

possible effects of the herb so he refused it, but his fellows took it.   It affected their minds and they ate a lot of food increasing their weight.   The inhabitants were cannibals and wanted to fatten the sailors to eat them. Students are sometimes made prey by drug dealers.

SINDBAD REFUSING HERBS =   CONTROL OF SITUATION

Sindbad refusing the herbs was able to retain his normal weight, and with enough freedom he escaped the cannibals and went to a nearby island.   He abandoned the course and the area of temptation.

MARRIAGE AT NEW ISLAND =   ENROLLING IN NEW COURSE

He was welcomed to the new island where he was accepted and began a career of work during which he met a woman he married and settled down. Began a new course of study.

BURIAL WITH DEAD SPOUSE =   NOT ALOWED TO COMPLETE NEW COURSE

In time one of his new friends was found to be in great distress. On inquiry Sindbad learned his friend was distressed because his wife had died and it was the custom of the country to bury a spouse with the dead. Not allowed to change course of study.

LOWERED INTO BURIAL CAVE = CONTEMPLATING SUICIDE

Sindbad had not long to realize his greatest fear, for his wife died and he was condemned to be buried with her.   In spite of his protests he was compelled to be lowered into the burial cave with his dead spouse.   He had some food given him so he was able to subsist for some days, but he knew he would soon starve to death in the cave. The course would soon be finished and there would be no other one to take.

FOLLOWING CREATURE TO FIND WAY OUT = TAKING ADVICE

Sindbad was feeling quite desperate but kept alert for some chance to escape.   One day he noticed a flow of air from somewhere and heard a creature come into the cave from a hidden opening.   He followed the animal and found the opening , permitting him to escape.   It was not far to the seashore and he was able to signal a passing ship and was rescued and eventually reached home again.   He had to leave to find a place he could continue his studies.

Fifth Voyage

STOP AT DESERT ISLAND =   STARTING NEW COURSE

Sindbad again decided to undertake a voyage with the usual trading goods to sell when he reached other countries. He had his own ship built and invited other merchants to join him.   They made good progress and as soon as they reached an island they decided to take shore leave and a rest.   They needed to know if there were studies available they could pursue.

EGG OF ROKH READY TO HATCH =   COURSE OF STUDY

On the island they found a large rokh egg ready to hatch.   Sindbad recognized the possible danger of meddling with the rokh's egg but his companions did not.   The course did not appear suitable.

KILLING AND ROASTING THE HATCHLING = UNCONTROLLABLE COMPANIONS DECIDING AGAINST THE   COURSE

Sindbad's companions unaware of the danger decided against his wishes to cook and eat the hatchling, quite large enough to feed a number of people.   The students were against taking the course but they wanted to try it.

FURY OF ROKHS DESTROYING SHIP = STUDENTS REJECTED BY AUTHORITIES

They were all surprised at the arrival of the two rokh parents quite annoyed at the destruction of their young.   The great birds proceeded to pick up large rocks in their claws and bombard the ship, destroying it and sinking it with all its crew who had tried to escape. Only Sindbad saved his life by clinging to wreckage and eventually getting back to the island.   He alone was allowed to take the course.

ISLAND WITH PLENTY OF FRUITS = COURSE WORTH TAKING

Sindbad found the island was quite a pleasant place with plenty of fruits to eat and he wandered about to explore it.   He was pleased with the course.

OLD MAN CLINGING TO BACK = ADDICTION

On his way around Sindbad saw an old man sitting beside a stream he was unable to cross.   He decided to help him and took the old man on his back across the stream. But when they reached the other side the old man would not get off his back, and clung to him even when night came and he had to rest,   and for several days later. A hanger-on or addiction can be a problem.

RUSE TO GET RID OF OLD MAN = WAY TO GET OUT OF THE ADDICTION

How to get rid of the old man was a problem.   He hit on a plan which was to take some of the fruits and let them ferment to produce an alcohol he gave the old man to drink.   This made the old fellow drunk and Sindbad was able to finally shake him off. Some people he met at the seashore told him he was fortunate for the old man had strangled some others.   He was invited to join their ship and set sail for home. He was able rid himself of a craving for alcohol and to finish the course.

SHIP HEADING FOR DESOLATE COAST = HAVING TO TAKE UNWANTED COURSE

Still wishing for adventure and trading possibilities, Sindbad set out on another trip with a group of merchants. Their ship was making good progress when the captain suddenly came to them and said they were caught in currents carrying them to a desolate coast where they were likely to be wrecked. No way to avoid it. The students were being forced to take a course they didn't want.

NO ESCAPE FROM COAST OF DEAD AND WRECKAGE = NO WAY TO GET OUT OF UNWANTED COURSE

As the captain had warned them, the ship finally was dashed against the rocks of a desolate coast and completely wrecked. They all escaped to the shore and were able to disembark with much of their merchandise and food,   but they were then stranded with no known way of escape.

LAUNCH OF RAFT OF LAST RESORT WITH TAKEN JEWELS = WAY OUT IF SOME OF COURSE TAKEN

Over the course of some months the food they had was all consumed and there was no recourse but to starve. Only Sindbad was able to survive the last of the crew because he was able to forage for some sea plants and animals and had eaten sparingly of the food he possessed. He was now alone and looked for some way of egress from the desolate spot. The cliffs around were not able to be climbed for their steepness, but he found a stream that entered a cave in the cliffs not noticed before. He built a raft that could pass through the cave opening and with the last of his provisions and taking jewels the other merchants had left, lay in the raft and let the stream carry him he knew not where.

WITH RAFT ENTERING CAVE ASLEEP = UNPLANNED LIFE PURSUIT

It was pitch dark in the cave and Sindbad slept off and on for several days as he was swept along, barely subsisting on the small amount of food he had kept. He did not know how the course would end or what he would do afterwards.

ARRIVING IN STRANGE COUNTRY = STARTING NEW JOB

Suddenly he woke up one day to find himself in daylight and in a strange country. His first request was for food, and the people in the strange country came to help him and took him to the ruler of their country. He offered the jewels he had to the ruler, but he was made welcome and instead given great gifts by the ruler who promised to help him reach his home. He could now get out of the course, and was allowed to graduate with new qualifications.

GOING BACK HOME WITH GIFTS = RESUMING USUAL LIFE PURSUIT

Sindbad was given passage on a ship leaving port and in time reached his home. He was able to take the gifts of considerable value to his Sultan. Take a good job.

ALADDIN OR THE WONDERFUL LAMP

ALADDIN = STUDENT (ADVANCED)

In this myth Aladdin could be considered an advanced student studying independently. His father had died -- end of supervision -- and his mother was worried that he contributed little to their living obligations.

AFRICAN MAGICIAN = DISTINGUISHED PROFESSOR

The magician could be a professor who wished to become associated with Aladdin. Professors profit by being associated with bright students. He said he was an uncle of Aladdin and brought him gifts and visited his home. Later he arranged for them to go out together to see gardens and the sights of the city.

MAGICAL DISCLOSURE OF UNDERGROUND CHAMBER= INTRODUCTORY TEACHING OF PRINCIPLES

Aladdin and the magician wandered outside the city to a secluded mountainous area where the magician performed a ritual fire-making and said some magic words revealing an opening to an underground chamber. He asked Aladdin to go down into the room where in an alcove he would find a lamp he must bring out. But on the way he would pass hanging jewels of exceptional brilliance he must not touch. On his way back he might take any of the jewels he wished but to bring the lamp.

He gave Aladdin a magic ring for protection.   This was an introductory course of study.

BRILLIANT FRUITS IN CHAMBER =
OUTSTANDING IDEAS

The fruits or hanging jewels were outstanding. Aladdin took as many as he could carry in his robes or pockets and the lamp in his bosom. He had a lot to remember from this preliminary study.

LAMP IN CHAMBER = KNOWLEDGE TO BE
LEARNED

Aladdin had found the lamp in the place the magician had described. It was lighted but he put it out and headed for the exit after gathering the jewels.   He knew there was still a lot to learn.

REFUSING TO GIVE UP LAMP = WANTING TO
LEARN INDEPENDANTLY

Before Aladdin could make his exit, and as he climbed up the ladder to the opening,   the magician asked him to hand out the lamp.   Aladdin couldn't hand out the lamp that easily because of the many jewels he carried, and protested that he could give up the lamp as soon as he got out.   The magician was annoyed by this, and impatiently threw some powder on the fire and the trapdoor closed leaving Aladdin in the dark. The professor was impatient with his student and felt he was wasting his time helping him.

THE MAGIC RING = INTRODUCTORY STUDIES

Aladdin lay at the bottom of the ladder wondering what he could do. Some time passed and may have run into days. Aladdin was becoming quite hungry and thirsty and feeling desperate at his imprisonment. He even felt he might be about to end his life and folded his hands to say his last prayers. But as he did so he rubbed the ring the magician had given him and in a flash of light a huge genie appeared asking what his wishes were. Aladdin suddenly had an idea.

GENIE OF THE RING = WHAT THESE STUDIES CAN ACCOMPLISH

Aladdin was greatly surprised at the appearance of the genie of the ring, but immediately asked him to get him out of the awful predicament he was in. At once the genie took him out into the open air. He saw the city in the distance and hurried towards it and soon reached home. The idea worked.

GENIE OF THE LAMP = WHAT ADVANCED KNOWLEDGE CAN DO

His mother was overjoyed to see him return; she had been so worried. He asked her for food because he was almost starved. She replied there was no food left in the house, but she would go out to buy some if she had something to sell. He gave her the lamp, but it looked old and needed to be shone to fetch as much money as possible. She got a rag to shine it. As soon as she rubbed the lamp, however, a huge genie appeared in a clap of thunder demanding what was wanted in a loud voice.

She swooned in fright,　but Aladdin grabbed the lamp and asked the genie to bring them food.　In a short time it was provided.　Aladdin found they could get anything they wanted as well as food by summoning the genie of the lamp at any time.　Using knowledge can get you by.

FOOD BROUGHT BY THE GENIE = SUSTENANCE FROM WORK DONE

Aladdin and his mother were therefore well-provided for in the days and months that followed. Aladdin also found he could sell the golden dishes the food was brought in.　The merchants who bought the dishes also taught Aladdin about metals and jewellery which comprised their trade.　Aladdin learned a lot in this way.

PRINCESS BADROULBOUDOUR = THEME FOR AN ADVANCED TREATISE

During Aladdin's activities in the city he heard one day about the daughter of the Sultan people were not allowed to look on even in her visits to the baths of the city.　Aladdin was curious and wished to see her himself, and hid until she passed by and he could get a glimpse of her.　He was immediately struck by her beauty.　He hadn't seen any woman's face except his mother's before this and was entranced.　More new ideas come his way.

REQUEST TO MARRY PRINCESS = PERMISSION TO WRITE A THESIS

Aladdin now felt an overwhelming desire to marry the princess.　He recognized he had immense power through the use of the genie of the lamp, and he had been able, through association with merchants and others in the city, to absorb the culture of the society he lived in and felt worthy of even a princess. His mother was not convinced and laughed at his presumptions. He knew what he wanted to do.

INTERSESSION BY MOTHER = REQUEST TO AUTHORITY BY PROMOTER

Aladdin had to have a sponsor for such a request of the Sultan, and prevailed on his mother to do it for him. She knew she had to have a great gift to make intercession to a Sultan, and Aladdin assured her the jewels he had brought from the underground garden would be sufficient. He knew the value of the knowledge and wanted to make use of it.

SULTAN AND VIZIER = AUTHORITY FIGURES

Aladdin's mother went to the palace of the Sultan and waited for some days to get an audience. She came and waited for several days and was finally recognized and asked what her mission was.

BASIS OF GRANTING WISH = BRILLIANT IDEAS (GEMS)

When she told the Sultan and his Vizier that Aladdin's wish was to marry the Princess, they were reluctant even to consider a low-born person to be such a suitor. However, they were amazed at the beauty and great worth of the jewels she had brought as a gift to them, and reconsidered the request. To make it more difficult for Aladdin they further requested a great quantity of the same kind of jewels and an elaborate method of presentation before his request could be granted. This Aladdin could provide with the help of the genie of the lamp. He had the knowledge to make his presentation.

VIZIER'S SON WANTS MARRIAGE TO PRINCESS = COMPETITION FROM OTHER STUDENT

The Vizier on the other hand had a son he wished the princess to marry so he could succeed to the office of Sultan in the future. He therefore prevailed on the Sultan to allow this marriage to happen before Aladdin's time of appointment could take place. The rival student takes advantage.

USING GENIE TO THWART VIZIER'S SON = USING KNOWLEDGE TO SHOW GREATER COMPETENCY

Aladdin heard accidentally about the hurried marriage and saw he could be disappointed by the machinations of the Vizier and his son. He again appealed to the Genie of the Lamp to carry out his instructions to not allow the consummation of the marriage. On the day of the marriage the Genie brought both the bride and groom to a place specified by Aladdin and the groom was held in a storeroom all night. When this was repeated a second day, the Vizier's son requested the marriage be dissolved, so the Princess was free.

MARRIAGE TO PRINCESS = PERMISSION TO BEGIN THESIS

The time for the Sultan to accede to Aladdin's request for marriage to the Princess soon came and his wish was granted. Aladdin was overjoyed but assured the Sultan he wished to build a glorious castle to accommodate the princess before the marriage, and this he could do in a very short time. He already had a plan of the thesis.

MAGNIFICENT CASTLE = THESIS

Aladdin again called on the Genie of the Lamp to build the castle and this was accomplished according to his instructions in a very short time. The marriage to the Princess was then performed and Aladdin and the Princess lived in the castle in great happiness.

MAGICIAN CARRIES OFF CASTLE AND PRINCESS = PROFESSOR CLAIMS THESIS AS HIS OWN WORK

Meanwhile the African Magician had news of the success of Aladdin, and suspecting the cause of all this achievement, he came to the country where the castle had been built. Through a ruse of exchanging new lamps for old the magician was able to obtain the Wonderful Lamp of the Genie. He immediately caused the castle and the Princess to be carried off to his domain in Africa. The professor gains control of the thesis and its possible publication.

ALADDIN USES GENIE OF RING TO REACH MAGICIAN = USE OF INTRODUCTORY STUDIES TO CLAIM OWNERSHIP OF THESIS

Aladdin was devastated by the disappearance of his castle and the Princess. He was under duress from the Sultan who deplored exceedingly his daughter's disappearance. Aladdin was in despair and as he walked by a river he felt like drowning himself. He folded his hands in prayer and in doing so rubbed the magic ring he still had on his finger. Immediately the Genie of the ring appeared to do his bidding. He assured Aladdin he didn't have the power to bring back the castle and the Princess, but he could take him to where they were in Africa.

PRINCESS HELPS ALADDIN TO KILL MAGICIAN = PROOF OF THESIS OWNERSHIP (ORIGINALITY OF THEME)

Aladdin made his presence known to the Princess when he arrived, and they made plans to dispose of the Magician as soon as possible and recover the lamp. Aladdin bought poison the Princess could put in the Magician's drink when he importuned her to give way to him as he did every day since their arrival. She succeeded in this and obtained the magic Lamp carried in his bosom when he died from the poison.

RETURN OF CASTLE AND PRINCESS = RECOGNITION OF ORIGINALITY OF THESIS

Aladdin and the Princess called on the Genie of the Lamp to bring them and the castle back to the palace of the Sultan who welcomed them with great joy, and Aladdin was restored to favour.

GENIE = POWER OF KNOWLEDGE

The genie of the lamp or the ring represents the power of knowledge one may possess to get things done. In Arabian mythology the names "ifrit" and "jinn" are also names of beings with magical powers indicating known technology one could employ when needed.

ALI BABA = KNOWING, RESOURCEFULNESS

The 'Open Sesame' used by Ali Baba was his ability to remember what he had learned, so he could enter the storage place of the thieves and leave when he wanted to. His brother Cassim did not have this facility and so lost his life when the thieves found him in their cave.

MORGIANA = CLEVERNESS, SKILL

Morgiana was the servant girl of Ali Baba's household. She recognized the schemes of the captain of the thieves who sought to kill Ali Baba, and foiled his attempts by destroying his men he had hidden in jars and had planned to use in an attack on Ali Baba. She eventually killed the captain when he was enjoying the hospitality of Ali Baba but had a concealed dagger to kill him.

"OPEN SESAME" = KNOWLEDGE AND ITS APPLICATION

To "know" something it is necessary not only to "learn" it but to apply it correctly. Or, we do not know anything unless we have also put it to work. Ali Baba learned and applied the "open sesame" correctly, but his brother, Cassim, did not learn sufficiently well the formula, so failed to apply it correctly. "A little learning is a dangerous thing" could be applied to his case. The thieves found him in their cave and murdered him.

A CONVERSATION

"Mornin', Youb."

"Mornin, Jim".

"Another book?"

"Yeah! Leftovers from the other two, I guess"

"A lot of Greek stuff!"

"I guess it's well known as mythology. Characters from modern stories or other literature would be probably less well known.   The Bible is less recognized as mythology, don't you think?"

"Ah, yes! I expect so. What's this about God?"

"I thought you'd ask that. Wise people of long ago had a name for something that existed and was very powerful and so on. They called it God. The idea changed very much over the years."

"But isn't (wasn't) God a personage in the sky or wherever?"

"That seems a common idea.   The real meaning, though, seems to be something more basic. It took me more than eighty years   to figure it out!"

"The meaning that "God" means "Life?""

"Yeah. I'm not the first to say so, you know. It's in the Bible for one.   John!" (Also the philosophers Bergson and Nietzche).

"Oh. I didn't see it. So now you believe in God, as they say".

"Well, I have to believe in Life. It's all around us, and in us. Very powerful and mysterious. In plants and animals 'til the end!"

"You're a smart cookie, Youb!"

"Not so smart, Jim. Eighty years! Sure takes a long time to figure things out! I have to call that slow! What do you say?"

"I expect you won't be believed!"

"Any more questions?"

ACKNOWLEDGEMENMTS

I appreciate the assistance of Julian Squires with computer programs and early transfer of the manuscript to the publishers. Craig Squires read part of an earlier version and I appreciate his comments. I appreciate also his help with computer procedures.

BIBLIOGRAPHY

BULFINCH, T. 1998. Bulfinch's Mythology. 862 p. The Modern Library, New York.

CAMPBELL, J. 1949. The Hero with a thousand faces. 415 p. Bollingen Series, Princeton Univ. Press, Princeton.

CAMPBELL, J. 1973. Myths to live by. 287 p. Bantam New Age Book. New York.

CHEVALIER, J. AND A. GHEERBRANT, Trans. by J. BUCHANAN-BROWN. 1994. Dictionary of Symbols. 1174 p. Penguin Books, London.

GRAVES, R. 1955. The Greek Myths. Vols I and II 782 p. Penguin Books. Harmondsworth, UK.

GRIMAL, P. 1963. Larousse World Mythology. Trans. by Patricia Beardsworth. 560 p. Hamlyn Publishing , London, UK.

LIPTZIN, S. 1985. Biblical themes in world literature. Ktav Publishing House, Inc. Hoboken, N. J. 316 p.

SQUIRES, H. J. 1996. Mythology for you. 208 p. Jesperson Press, St. John's, NL, Canada.

SQUIRES, H. J. 2003. Survival stories from mythology. 223 p. ESP Press, Portugal Cove, NL, Canada.

INDEX OF NAMES

The Symbol

When he was young, he found deep in his mind
      An abstract shape. It took form once in the sand
Where a meditative finger tried a simple scrawl;
      But it struck deep down, re-echoed often in his
          dreams,
And fathered deeds, or so he thought – his chops upon
          the beams
To mark accomplishments: triumphs in the Hall of
          Genes.

Abstractions made by humans are characters of Mind;
Shapes uplifting from lowly primeval things (earth
          binding).
The Symbol bore a gift of power to spur his kind:
To break through clouds of doubt, restraint and chiding.
Shining in the turbulence gave it wealth of meaning,
          leading on
To self-fulfillment, worthy of his strength and Being.

But the workings of events of chance brought down to
          earth
The naked Symbol: crushed, tarnished, broken and
          deformed:

Or so he thought. And he bowed despondent and in grief
to where the Symbol lay:
The broken dream, longed-for relief could help no more
the plateaued life,
A time of thought decay. How to break the chains that
cling – dull habit and delusion --
Unworthy of his strengths and being.

Then, then he looked for Reason, abstractions that no
symbols need – no need
Of god-god or devil-god to pose a way to break from poor
inaction.
Clear was the way as the Symbol faded, no more its need
for aspirations.
The mind itself broke free to search and find its own true
inspirations.
Abstract they might be but full of meaning, turning the
symbols to realities
Essential to his being.

-- Hubert Squires, 1965

www.ingramcontent.com/pod-product-compliance
Lightning Source LLC
Chambersburg PA
CBHW020307290526
45784CB00003B/1403